T0137634

$\mathcal{L}$ove That Works

The 12 Foundation Stones:

A Success Plan For Long-Term Committed Love Relationships

Saundra Dickinson

North America & international
toll-free: 1 888 232 4444 (USA & Canada)
phone: 250 383 6864 ♦ fax: 812 355 4082

Order this book online at www.trafford.com
or email orders@trafford.com

Most Trafford titles are also available at major online book retailers.

In this book, all the details and circumstances about peoples'
lives in this book have been fictionalized.

No "client" or other person that is mentioned corresponds to any actual person,
living or dead (with the exception of the author's life experience).

Additionally, the information printed herein is not intended to be considered
counseling or other professional advice by the publisher or author.

The views expressed in this work are solely those of the author and do not necessarily reflect
the views of the publisher, and the publisher hereby disclaims any responsibility for them.

Printed in the United States of America.

ISBN: 978-1-4269-4220-4 (sc)
ISBN: 978-1-4269-4214-3 (e)

Trafford rev. 02/21/2011

 www.trafford.com

North America & international
toll-free: 1 888 232 4444 (USA & Canada)
phone: 250 383 6864 ♦ fax: 812 355 4082

Acknowledgements

First and foremost, I am grateful and indebted to Harville Hendrix, Ph. D. and Helen LaKely Hunt, Ph. D., co-authors of, Getting the Love You Want: A Guide for Couples; Keeping the Love You Find: A Guide for Singles; and Giving the Love That Heals: A Guide for Parents. Their amazing knowledge, wisdom, and insight into long-term, committed love relationships, and their marvelous ability to make this information sensible and manageable offer couples a positive, logical, non-threatening path to follow as they work to put their marriages on a new track.

All my work with couples and families is based on the IMAGO theory, created, defined, and developed by these two pioneering therapists. Without their understanding and clarification around long-term, committed love relationships, I myself would not be celebrating 47 years of marriage, nor would my three grown daughters have the relationships they now have with my husband and me, their own husbands, and their precious children.

Beyond the vital importance for my practice of the IMAGO theory and work of Harville Hendrix and Helen Hunt, I owe a debt of gratitude to numerous others as well. I appreciate Joyce Buckner for her unfailing patience, friendship, and compassion as my teacher and mentor throughout my IMAGO training. It took Joyce's remarkable intelligence and unique ability to teach me the principles of this theory, and she continues to assist me with insights into its magnitude. So often, I hear her voice in my head explaining some aspect I had completely missed, or passed over so quickly that I failed to take in its full importance.

Martha Baldwin Beveridge has been a constant support and unfailing encouragement to my desire and intention to write this book. An author herself, Martha has given me a role model for overcoming the hesitations and stuck thinking that can beset someone undertaking to write a first book. Her belief in me has been unlimited and gave me the courage to begin and finish this project.

More thanks and appreciation for the constant love and support of my family, including my husband, three daughters and their husbands, and my sister who actually bought a computer compatible with mine in order to transcribe for me, so that on visits I could use hers interchangeably with my own laptop.

My friends have been tirelessly patient, listening to all my tribulations as I've worked on the book and helping me "clear the cobwebs out of my brain" by means of periodic bridge games and various outings.

Without the input, patience, encouragement, and support of my editor, Betsy Tice White, this work would have never come together into a book form. She has been my faithful cheerleader and steady beacon who has kept me moving on this project throughout countless life interruptions. Her own psychological discernment pulled us out of many a ditch to get us up and moving again. From the very first conversation I had with Betsy, the feeling was right, and she held true to her early words to me that we would make our book. She has been a joy to work with, a pleasure to know as a fellow human being interested in writing, intelligent, and a solid Southern woman of values. Thank you again, Betsy, for all your contributions to this effort.

Contents

Introduction

I haven't been a therapist all my adult life, but I have been in relationships all my life, and I'm continually amazed at how many millions of us pair off with someone we genuinely love, get married, have children or not, then ultimately see our primary love relationship deteriorate into a numbed-out co-existence, become mired in addictions that will eventually destroy it, or end in divorce.

Nor have my husband of 47 years and I been immune to such difficulties. Along our own turbulent journey, we've been blessed with ample opportunities to grow up and learn what we need to know to make our marriage endure. High-school sweethearts, we now have three grown daughters and eight grandkids. Looking at what was passed down to us in the way of dealing with life, we see clearly that we passed on to our children and even their children many of the lessons we learned in childhood, some of them far from helpful to anyone wanting healthy, connected relationships.

In fact, the most preparation any of us have for this major part of our lives called marriage and family is what we experienced in our own families of origin. A few fortunate ones among us may say, "I only hope my marriage can be as strong and loving as my parents' was." But too many of us learned unhealthy and dysfunctional patterns of relating to those we love.

It's as if we're given the task of driving a standard-shift automobile with no clear instructions, no manual, and no positive personal experience to guide us—only an imaginary picture in our minds of what driving a car should be like. So "doing marriage" has been a form of uneducated, unsupervised, on-the-job training.

Imagine that you've never driven a car yourself, and the only people you've ever ridden with had wrecks or near-wrecks. Nobody ever mentions the specifics necessary for maintaining an automobile, such as gas, oil, water, rotating tires, battery, transmission fluid, etc. Nor does anyone tell you anything about shifting gears, letting the clutch in or out, or applying the accelerator or the brakes. Certainly no one ever mentions a look in the rearview mirror, which could help you see where you're coming from. So even if you can figure out how to get the monster going, chances are that at some point you'll crash and burn, or narrowly miss doing so.

To me that's a perfect example of the way our society goes at marriage—no clear information, no manual, no competency requirements, and very limited personal experience that can lead to positive, healthy outcomes for us, our partners, and our children. Society's distressing statistics on marriage and divorce let us know how poorly we're doing, if left to our own devices.

Being able to sustain and enjoy long-term, committed, love relationships calls, I believe, for significant education and learned, practical skills. When couples or families come to my office to work on their relationships, I begin teaching them what I'm calling the **Twelve Foundation Stones,** so that they can begin building a **love that works.**

These are certainly not my original thoughts or discoveries. Most of my relationship work is based on the IMAGO theory of Harville Hendrix, Ph.D., and Helen LaKelly Hunt, Ph. D. The Twelve Foundation Stones are, however, a simple way of identifying the underlying dynamics that can do great damage to our relationships or even destroy them, if we remain unaware of them and their effects. And we need this awareness in order to benefit from the positive potential that lies within these Foundation Stones.

Although I began writing this book to assist my clients in their therapeutic work, I've come to see its broader application to anyone wanting a healthier, more enduring marriage. It's become clear to me how much our society romanticizes and mystifies love—so much so that very few of us know how to sustain a long-term connected relationship when the "good stuff" of Romantic Love evaporates, to be replaced by the Power Struggle's pain.

We have difficulty associating *work* and *effort* with love, because our definition of love between two partners is so heavily loaded with only the romantic version. Generally, partners wreck their marriages, then one or the other concludes that he or she has "been hurt so much that the damage is irreparable." Blaming our partner for the wounding is much easier than recognizing and acknowledging that we, too, have been doing considerable damage of our own.

The purpose of this book, then, is to help partners understand in practical and simple language how they hurt one another—usually without intending to—how to stay connected through the rough times, and how to work through their differences, instead of bailing out, shutting down, and retreating into a frozen reactive stance.

Success of any long-term, committed love relationship requires both partners to understand certain patterns and specific dynamics that will eventually appear in any sustained, committed love relationship. I've used my own journey in a long-term marriage and the experiences of the hundreds of couples I have worked with to compile these basic dynamics as I see them, as well as practical models for working with them once they are identified in the relationship.

My hope is that this enlightenment of the **Twelve Foundation Stones** will give couples a head start in restructuring their relationship, to make it the one they have always wanted. Along with my work as a therapist, teacher, and guide, I offer my formal education and training as a Certified IMAGO Relationship Therapist and Workshop Presenter, years of facilitating relationship therapy, and the ongoing "laboratory" of my own marriage as my husband and I work to live this theory ourselves.

I welcome the challenge and opportunity this work provides, for if we know all the systems operating—the **Twelve Foundation Stones**—we can better master the whole course. My book is designed as a starting point for understanding these dynamics. I hope to inspire and motivate those in long-term relationships who feel stuck, trapped, unfulfilled—those couples who are in or just beginning relationship therapy, and others who for one reason or another are seeking solutions on their own.

What are these twelve crucial Foundation Stones? The chapter titles in the Table of Contents list the names of them all. And as you begin to read and explore, I hope that you'll consider this an opportunity to start anew and carve out with your partner the marriage you have always wanted.

Chapter 1

The Power of the Unconscious Mind

"What in the world made me do that?"

We are aware of only a certain percentage of our brain's stored content at any given time. No one knows for sure the exact percentage, but let's assume about ten percent and label that our Conscious Mind.

We "know" everything that is in our Conscious Mind and have easy access to it. We can add to its content and draw from it whenever we want, as if it's a massive reference library. This part of our brain contains all the information and data we need on any regular basis. It stores our personal history and memories, as well as how to do our jobs and assorted tasks, count money, peel potatoes, sing, draw, play an instrument, drive a car, take someone's temperature, do the multiplication tables, plan a vacation, and thousands of other tasks that we routinely do.

Our brains are sophisticated enough to take all that stored data and help us work with it, organizing it into thoughts, plans, and rational thinking. When working out of our Conscious Mind, we are very predictable and can multi-task without putting much thought into the processes. I can talk on the phone, for example, while composing my grocery list, putting in a load of laundry, or changing a diaper. I can watch television and work a crossword puzzle at the same time.

When we're operating out of our Conscious Mind, everyone likes us better, because we're predictable and therefore perceived as emotionally safer. We do what appears rational and orderly, thus seeming relatively safer to those around us. We appear to be in control of ourselves and our situation, or at least responding logically and rationally to it.

Conscious Mind and work. The Conscious Mind is the part of our brain we use when we're task oriented, and of course we're most predictable when we're at work. In the work context, other people find us relatively easy to talk to and try to get to know, which makes them feel safer in our company. At work most of us try to keep our best foot forward—do a good job—because doing a good job benefits us, and in order to do a good job, we have to remain as predictable and in control as possible, even in moments of conflict or crisis. At work, unless we are mentally unhinged, we avoid upsetting others or behaving in scary ways. If we're thinking about our job security, we probably never throw fits, speak disrespectfully to others, or pout. The boss or CEO might do those things, but not us ordinary working folk.

Therefore, no matter if we work in an office, an operating room, or a stockroom, we're continually crafting a picture of ourselves, whether we realize it or not, that convinces our co-workers any interactions with us will be emotionally safe. This self-portrait we create encourages those around us to believe that dealing with us will remain safe—not upsetting or scary. Our co-workers learn to expect us not to act like loose cannons. They believe they know us and trust that working with us will be okay.

Why am I making this connection between the Conscious Mind and work? It's because this predictability and feeling of emotional safety between us and our co-workers is the primary reason most affairs begin at work—with people we know or are getting to know. Both we and the majority of our co-workers behave in predictable, intentional ways, so that we feel safe emotionally with each other and *appear at our best*.

Conscious Mind's editing job. One of the Conscious Mind's main functions is to constantly edit all incoming and outgoing information to fit our realities, so that we remain comfortable with the information. All of us prefer to know about and remember *pleasant* information, experiences, and feelings, rather than *unpleasant* ones. Unpleasantness feels burdensome and tends to weight us down emotionally, whereas pleasantness is lighter, something we enjoy sharing with others. So, we edit our unpleasant feelings and information, massaging or rearranging them until they're in a form we can tolerate with less discomfort.

Suppose, for example, someone says to me, " Saundra, you really look mad."

I might reply, "No, I'm not mad. I might be a little upset, but I'm certainly not mad."

See how I rearranged the words and information to make us both more comfortable with the reality? The result of this editing process burrows into the Conscious Mind, so that later on we accept this edited or doctored version of what happened as our truth and reality. And edited versions of what happened can stay with us for most of our lives.

Any number of motivations might provoke me to perform these little mental acrobatics. Maybe I think being mad isn't a nice way to be, so I work with my feelings and name them something else, in order to feel better about myself and my state of mind. Or maybe I'm afraid the other person won't approve or will get upset if I admit I really am mad, so I water the "mad" down to become "upset." Or maybe I was never taught or encouraged to claim my true feelings, because I never lived with people who allowed themselves to do so honestly.

We edit our memories so that we can tolerate them more comfortably. It's common to hear people speak of "getting over" or "moving past" some unpleasant experience or memory. We work on our opinions, hopes, beliefs, and values to arrange them into a shape that is suitable and comfortable for us, given our history and experience of life. We also work on our opinions, hopes, beliefs, etc., in an effort to make sense of or justify them.

Editing our conscious behaviors. The behaviors that we edit in our Conscious Mind are those that we *intend* to do—intentional behaviors that we have thought out, planned, and expect to carry out rationally. Suppose, for example, that you've made a 3:00 p.m. appointment to see me for a therapy session a few days hence. In order to keep that appointment, you'll devise a plan that allows you to arrive at my office no later than 3:00 p.m. on the stated day.

It may take considerable planning—asking off from work, getting a sitter for your child, making sure your car has enough gas, leaving home early enough to beat the traffic. Or, if something comes up a day or two before the appointment that means you aren't going to be able to see me at the appointed time, you call me at least 24 hours ahead of time to let me know you can't make it.

In either case, that's rational, thought-out, planned behavior. It's predictable, not scary or threatening. We prefer to behave in this predictable, rational manner ourselves, and everyone around us prefers it also. It just makes the wheels of life run smoother.

We find we're able to behave in this predictable way most of the time, unless a situation arises in which our emotions take over. And there's greater likelihood of that happening when we have a heavy emotional investment in a particular person or situation.

Enter the Unconscious Mind. This editing process I've described is also affected by the Unconscious Mind, where the *un*edited portion of our history is stored, though we're only aware of the edited part that lies in the Conscious Mind. It's vital to understand that everything an individual "knows" with his Conscious Mind about feelings, beliefs, values, and experiences is colored by the history and experiences stored in that person's Unconscious Mind, even though he is not aware of this influence. Because this is so, although we're all human beings, my personal reality is quite different from yours, and your personal reality is quite different from that of everyone else. Regardless of our human similarities, each one of us has a uniquely personal view of the world.

No one knows, really, how all this happens, although we can make an attempt to describe the process. It begins with the arrival of data or information in our brain—what we actually see, hear, smell, taste, are told, read, feel. As these stimuli arrive, they pass through both our Conscious and Unconscious Minds, where they mix with our edited and unedited history and experiences of life.

At that point, some of the information will then be filtered back into our Conscious Mind. By the time this information arrives back at our Conscious Mind, colored by our stored history and previous life experience, it may no longer resemble what originally came into our brain.

Think about what happens when you pour water into a glass that formerly contained Easter-egg dye. Unless the glass has been thoroughly scrubbed out, the fresh water will show a tint of the old dye. So it is with information passing through the Conscious and Unconscious Minds. That old "egg dye" is in there, can't be scrubbed out, so the next "water" poured in will have some of that same tint. Therefore, what means one thing to one person will mean something entirely different to another. My "dye" will not be the same as yours.

All information or data received in a person's brain intermingles with that person's particularly unique collection of conscious and unconscious material about life and experience. We all like to imagine we have the same "truth"— the same reality—as everyone else, but that isn't so. Each of us thinks we hold the "real truth," because believing that feels predictable and safe for us. And if everyone else's "truth" matched our "truth," then there would be no room for misunderstandings in the world.

Even though we may speak the same language, have similar life experiences, or have grown up in the same family, no two of us experienced that family, those life experiences, or that language in the same way.

Conscious Mind's role in will power. The last important feature we need to look at in the Conscious Mind is will power. What we call will power is a conscious effort to make something happen, achieve some result. Our will power is part of our intent, and we may believe that if we *will* something strongly enough in any area of life, including a relationship, we can overcome any obstacle.

But that is not what happens. Something else is operating to interfere with our will power. Will power is just another form of intent, and it gets sabotaged in exactly the same way that our other "good" intentions get sabotaged. I'm not saying we shouldn't *have* good intentions or strong will power; however, when those fail us, which they surely will, at that point we need to try to understand the underlying forces that act to sabotage our plans, and instead of fighting them, learn to work with those energies so that we can understand our self-defeating behaviors and alter them.

Romantic Love and the Power Struggle. When we choose someone to marry, we intend to have a life of happiness with that partner, else we wouldn't bother to make such a huge commitment. Ultimately, however, what happens in a committed love relationship is quite different from how we imagined it when we were caught up in Romantic Love. The onset of the Power Struggle changes everything in our relationship.

If the only force operating in our brain were the 10% Conscious Mind, then whatever we intend to have happen in our lives would indeed happen. We would think, plan, and rationally carry out our intent. And wouldn't that be a picture-perfect Ward and June Cleaver life?

But as anyone who's been married can attest, that's not the way it works— not by a long shot. So something else must be operating that interferes with our conscious intent and will. That something else is our Unconscious Mind, the other 90% of our brain.

The Unconscious Mind revisited. We do not know what is in our Unconscious Mind, nor do we have willful and ready access to that part of our brain. The Unconscious Mind acts as a recorder and huge storage cabinet of everything that has touched our lives or any cell of our body, even since before birth. Its contents include any taste, smell, thought, touch, hope, dream, anything we have heard or experienced, seen in a movie, read in a book, learned in school—literally anything that has come in contact with us or any cell of our bodies. Nothing escapes the scrutiny of the Unconscious Mind's sensor screens. The amount of material recorded and held in the Unconscious Mind is massive, so much so that if we had to be aware of or "know" all of it, we couldn't function or even get out of bed!

We lack direct awareness of this material because we do not have willful access to the Unconscious Mind. It remains a very protected part of us, and rightly so, because it protects our most vulnerable parts. The very protective nature of this system dictates that most of this material needs to remain undisturbed, unfelt, and unnoticed. Even so, some feelings and behaviors in this huge memory bank of the Unconscious Mind related to unfinished issues from our childhoods have never been brought to our awareness or validated consciously. And these unresolved issues from our childhood are the very ones that will be triggered in our present-day relationships where we want to feel connected to another person and loved by him or her.

Why must I revisit my childhood? People often stop me here and say, "Look, I'm having problems in my relationship *today*. I can't see any reason to go all the way back to childhood to help me understand the problems."

Here's my answer. For all of us who have reached adulthood, the only things I know of that remain unresolved are those things that happened to us in childhood, when our only options were to find ways to survive around the dysfunction. Parents can run the gamut from wonderful to terrible, but most families operate around dysfunction of one kind or another, and the children in those families have to figure out how to survive.

I agree with John Lee, a therapist in Austin, Texas, who states that life's only true victims are children. Although some adults may see themselves as victims, in reality there are no adult victims, because adults always have "car keys" of one kind or another. In other words, as adults, if life gets too tough for us, we can always use whatever "car keys" we have and "move on down the road." Couples can divorce if their relationship feels unbearable. Divorce may not be what they really want, but at least it provides some form of resolution.

But as children, we truly live at the mercy of the big folk in charge of our lives. Whatever they decide for us is what happens. Even if something ends by going our way, their decision allowed it to happen. So the only issues that remain unresolved in any of us as adults are matters about which we had no choice—things that happened at a time in our lives when we had very few options to help us survive.

Childhood themes always raise their heads. We may not "know" or have any conscious awareness of our need to come to emotional peace around these unresolved issues, but they keep trying to get our attention. It's exactly these unresolved childhood themes that often underlie our lack of work success, parenting difficulties, failed friendships or love relationships, and inability to love and trust ourselves, as well as others.

These issues "want" to be resolved, and they let us know that by seeping out into our relationships. "Now, look, Saundra," a client may say. "How can you say I need to deal with this unresolved stuff, when you can see how successful I am in my life?" It may be a doctor, lawyer, CPA, pilot, or any other successful professional talking. But their success has been in task performance, not relationships. The relationship arena seems to be the acid test. I suspect that that the higher we perform in the task arena of our lives, the lower we perform in our committed relationships. A high-functioning professional is probably putting more time, energy, and willingness into the work part of life than into relationships. And successful love relationships also require time and energy and willingness.

Task performance and relationship performance have different origins. As we noted earlier, the task portion of us—the intellectual, not so emotional part—is seated more in the Conscious Mind, because that information is needed on a daily basis. We are doing a job, operating in a concrete, black-and-white, factual world. Relationships, on the other hand, take place in our emotional world—the gray, vulnerable, not so intellectual part of us. In general, it's much easier to perform a memorized task (fill out a tax return, do surgery, state laws, cook) than to carry on a long-term, emotionally connected relationship.

I often tell clients, "If all I had to do was teach this work to couples, my life would be a piece of cake. For all of us, going home and living it on a day-to-day basis with a partner and a family is the hardest work any of us will ever do, but it also brings us the greatest rewards."

How to get to the Unconscious Mind. People often ask me, "If we have no awareness of what's in the Unconscious Mind, how can we get to that information?" Life has given us an amazing answer to that question. The answer actually comes from the *magical uniqueness* of the *Committed Love Relationship*—the relationship that exists when two persons who love each other commit their lives to one another, with the intent of staying together forever. The information we need in order to deal with the *seepage* that sabotages our relationships surfaces more clearly in the Committed Love Relationship than anywhere else.

When I committed my life and joined it to another's, I certainly wasn't thinking of it as the first step on the royal road to the Unconscious Mind, but that's exactly the opportunity such a relationship offers. Through the support and encouragement of another person who loves me, I can grow, slowly though sometimes painfully, into my most complete, evolved, and highest functioning self.

We cannot recognize nor decode our own unconscious agendas without the help of some other caring person, and in the best of circumstances that person will be our life partner. He or she experiences in us what we cannot see about ourselves, and, ideally, will *tell us* what that experience is. If my unconscious agenda dictates excessive control of others to help me feel safer in life, my partner will definitely pick up on that. If my partner lacks ambition, afraid to take appropriate initiative in his work, I will soon realize that. With the right spirit of honesty, openness, and willingness, we will find caring ways to share our perceptions with each other, in the interest of a fuller life together.

When your partner is being honest with you, listen! Whatever strategies we relied on in childhood to help us survive will make perfect sense to us, even now. We won't see them as unusual, odd, or dysfunctional. When my partner tries to point out my ways of surviving that intrude upon his or her life, my first reaction is to think my partner is "wrong" or "crazy," and I will probably say so. But this honest feedback is an opportunity for growth, if we will take it. If we learn to listen, take the information in, and try the new behaviors that the partner suggests for better ways of surviving, we will gain some valuable new life skills.

Suppose a workaholic spouse is on a driven path to perform. When the workaholic's spouse points out that fact, the workaholic will automatically resist the information, because a "strong work ethic" is the main strategy that person has devised to survive in life. The partner is probably suggesting, however, that if the relationship between the two of them is to improve, that way of surviving needs to be altered. At that moment, stuck in his or her unconscious agenda, the workaholic doesn't believe there is any better way to survive. So, *a new belief system* must be built, supported by faith in the dissatisfied partner's input, plus a willingness to stretch into new ways of operating.

We cannot change things of which we are unaware. The goal of discovery of our unconscious agenda is to bring what is unknown to us about our behaviors into consciousness, so that we can change behaviors that are hurtful to or discounting of others. As long as our unconscious agenda remains unknown to us, the hurtful behaviors attached to that agenda operate fully without our knowledge or permission. We are not making a conscious choice about whether to use those behaviors or not. Once we become aware of them, however, we can make a conscious choice about what to do with them.

Nicole is moody and has a tendency to sulk and withdraw when she is upset, instead of addressing whatever or whoever upset her. Niles, her husband, and her three sisters have pointed this out to her for most of her life. But Nicole doesn't really listen to them. "You're just exaggerating!" she says. "I'm not moody, I don't sulk." Finally, Niles insists on counseling so that he can more effectively and safely confront this behavior of Nicole's.

After several sessions and many actual examples from Niles, Nicole begins to listen with some dawning recognition that Niles may have a point. Once she consciously grasps the information Niles has been giving her about her behavior, she decides to watch herself and monitor how she behaves when upset. Plus, she gave Niles permission to point out calmly and gently when she failed to notice one of her hurtful behaviors. The outcome? With the help of Niles's input, Nicole makes a conscious choice to alter her way of expressing her upsetness and tells Niles about it, so he can be prepared and aware of recognizing it. They work out a plan where they can speak openly with each other about anything that's upsetting to either of them. Nicole learns to put language to her feelings and stops *acting them out* on Niles and the rest of her family.

If you have a partner who is willing to give you honest feedback about how he or she experiences you in the relationship, welcome the blessing that it can be! You are fortunate, and the likelihood is high that you are in a relationship that will give you the trust and love you've always wanted. Of course, in that Committed Love Relationship you must also be willing to give your partner the same information about how you experience his or her behavior. And both of you have to be willing to learn to deliver this information in a way that each of you can take it in, hear it, and alter your energy in ways that keep the relationship connected and healthy.

Sounds simple, doesn't it? I tell you how I experience you, you tell me how you experience me, and we all live happily ever after. And if the Unconscious Mind were not involved, it might work like that!

Unconscious feelings and behaviors. The feelings and behaviors arising from the Unconscious Mind are raw and unedited, the opposite of intentional. They are reactive, knee-jerk, primitive, survival behaviors, which can serve as messages to our partners that for some reason we are feeling emotionally (and sometimes physically) unsafe in the relationship. They are *reactions*, not *responses*. What kinds of reactions am I talking about? Angry outbursts, accusations, blaming, sulking, shutting down, crying, nagging, preaching, flouncing out of the room and slamming the door—those are just a few of the great variety in our repertoires.

When this reactive behavior breaks out, signaling that we are unsafe to our partner, he or she will also disconnect by using some version of their own reactivity. Each partner's reactive behaviors elicit greater reactivity from the other, and the situation will either escalate and get scary—which is a disconnect—or else one or both partners will withdraw altogether—which is also a disconnect.

In either case, both partners will be reactive and disconnected from the relationship, because they will be focused on surviving the emotional unsafety they are experiencing. At this point, one partner or both usually blames the other for the problems in the relationship, not realizing that an opportunity has arrived to look a little deeper, learn something useful, and grow. *This realization is a learned skill and will not happen instantly nor without a high level of awareness and intentional behavior.*

When we cool down, these are big questions that open the magic doors:

- For me to react so strongly around this topic, what might this be about for me?
- What is unfinished (still a raw nerve) in me that I would react so strongly?
- What is my unconscious trying to help me resolve around this topic?

Not surprisingly, the most frequent answer to these questions is a defensive and reactive one: "If my partner had not done X, Y, and Z, I wouldn't have had to do P, Q, and R!" The partner who falls back on blaming the other has missed out on the valuable opportunity to do some self-searching and learn something new about himself.

Neither partner can figure out who did what first to make the relationship unsafe, because all the "stuff" is coming up from the Unconscious Mind of both, and by now they can't focus on anything else but blaming the other. Actually, figuring out *who* did or said what to whom isn't the important thing. The *important* thing is for each partner to figure out *what* the other person said or did that caused such a strong reaction within themselves, and what raw nerve from each of their personal histories the action or the words struck.

Of course, *in a relationship no one operates in a vacuum.* Anyone who reacts is reacting to *something.* If my partner is reactive, *what am I doing* to make him or her feel unsafe enough to react with knee-jerk behavior? *What was my partner doing or saying* that felt unsafe enough to me to elicit my own knee-jerk reaction? Those are the questions we need to be asking ourselves, as calmly and thoughtfully as we can.

Most of us go the opposite direction: "See what you made me do? You're the one making me act this way!" But pointing fingers and blaming solves nothing, while it keeps the dance going.

The man or the woman in the mirror. At a place where regular Twelve-Step recovery meetings are held, I once noticed a big mirror in the hallway between the meeting rooms and restrooms. Above it were these words: "A PORTRAIT OF THE REAL PROBLEM." The portrait in that mirror is the starting place for all of us, at the moment we determine to get serious about forming healthy, connected relationships.

In such relationships, both partners are *willing to take ownership* of the problems and *be accountable* for whatever part they may have played in them. They are willing to listen when a partner reports the wounding effect of some word or action of the other. Not only are partners in a healthy relationship *willing to listen and take in what was said*, they are also *willing to alter their hurtful behavior* around this touchy point, *whether they agree or not about the touchy point.*

Intent is not all that matters. Human beings are not usually eager to hear about and own how hurtful their behavior can be, most especially if they *did not intend* it as hurtful. We want to rely on *our intent*, not someone else's input, as the barometer to let us know if we have been hurtful. It requires a huge but necessary growth leap to take responsibility for altering a behavior that we believe is totally harmless.

The astonishing power of words. For a humorous, but completely true example of how such interactions can work, at one time in my marriage I began noticing that every time my husband used the word "evidently," I felt my guts tighten up. I didn't know what that was about for me, but I knew enough to ask him to not use that word for a while until I could figure out what was trying to come to light.

We had already grown considerably in relationship issues, because years previously I wouldn't have been aware that the word "evidently" did anything to me, let alone ask him to not use it for a while. And in those days if I had made such a request, probably he'd have told me I was crazy to even try to dictate to him how he could talk.

Because we've both learned and grown a lot with each other, that day his response was, "Okay, but let me know when you have it figured out."

Believe me, specific words with roots in our past have power! It didn't take me long to settle back into mine and remember my dad using a particular word on me when he was angry and accusing me of some infraction of his rules—such as spilling my milk. That word was "deliberately." His assumption was that no matter what happened, I meant to mess up and was "deliberately" making his life miserable. His language was terribly hurtful for me, because with no defense against it, I came to view myself as he seemed to see me—an insensitive, unlovable ingrate who deserved his tyrannical "corrections."

And then I remembered that my husband's father did the same thing, only he used the word "evidently" to condemn anyone. He would ask, "Did you clean the car?" No matter how you answered, he would come back with, "Well, evidently you didn't, because . . . " His target, too, ended up tried, convicted, and verbally hung.

Somehow, these two words got cross-wired in my brain, so that every time I heard my husband use the word "evidently," my body told me I was a tried and convicted, horrible person who "deliberately" did mean things to others. Finally I saw the light, why his use of a simple word such as "evidently" caused such a strong reaction in me. When I revealed all of this to my husband, he could easily empathize with my sensitivity over these words, and we both ended up having a good laugh at how our brains work.

Why this story matters. This story is important because, in the past, before we began to credit the power of the Unconscious Mind,

1) None of this scenario would have ever been talked about,
2) I would have been afraid to mention his dad's part in it,
3) I would never have noticed my body and what it was trying to tell me,
4) I would have stayed silently angry and hurt at my husband, but wouldn't have consciously let myself know it,
5) The way our brains work in relationships would have never been discovered, discussed, or recognized, preventing us from circumventing other potentially toxic situations in our future together,
6) We would have said nothing and let the Unconscious Mind run and ruin our marriage—which it can do, if left undiscovered.

For those so adamantly opposed to looking back at their past, I pose these questions about this little interchange between my husband and me:

- What harm did we do? (None)
- Did we end up hating our parents? (No)
- Are we permanently scarred from this journey back into the past? (No)
- Where is the damage or the waste of time? (There is none)

So, taking the journey into the past actually did us a lot of good, took a minimum of time, and has given us both some awesome insight into the power of the Unconscious Mind and some fun moments with these two words, "evidently" and "deliberately." Even better, it moved us out of a potential gridlock of anger and mutually hurt feelings.

What did it take? For me, first, it took paying attention to my body and realizing the tightness in my gut, then speaking about it to my partner. For my husband, it took *holding the tension of his discomfort* about being told <u>not</u> to use a certain word, which meant almost nothing to him. Again, for me, it took a little time and willingness to discover what in my past was connected to that tightness in my gut. No big deal!

Everyone can duplicate this process, yet we spend enormous amounts of time and energy resisting this kind of *historical, unconscious* journey, instead of just doing it and reaping the benefits in our relationships.

Start small. Don't try to conquer the Big Kahuna of unresolved pain from your childhoods. You may be surprised to realize the amount of pain we still carry and try to get resolved from the lesser painful events from childhood, *i.e.*, a look, an attitude, a smirk.

The good news about the Unconscious Mind. Yes, there is good news about that oldest part of our brain. Very little of its massive content needs to be disturbed. I would guess that about five to ten percent awareness of its "stuff" is all we need to stop the seepage that disrupts our relationships. Even so, the more of our unconscious agenda we can access and pull into our consciousness, the healthier and more loving our relationships can become.

In the interest of clearing the way for these healthy, satisfying relationships, partners can benefit from a few basic steps to help with integrating information from the Unconscious into the Conscious Mind. Learning to live this new way with a partner takes work, but the rewards are more than worth it. Lawyers, mediators, judges, and divorce courts are a lot of work, too, and in the end can cost us a lot more than we bargained for. So here are the basic steps, remembering to use Intentional Dialogue (see Chapter 4 for the format) throughout this exercise:

1. Both partners ask for honest feedback from each other as to how the partner experiences them in their relationship. By honest feedback, I mean being *real* with each other. If you're not sure what that term means, check out Chapter 11 on Getting Real.

2. Both partners work with each other to deliver that feedback in a way that doesn't wound the other emotionally, so he or she can take it in and hear it.

3. Both partners become willing to alter their delivery/behavior in response to that feedback, as they are guided by their partner.

4. Both partners work with each other to manage their individual energies in the relationship, so that each one feels emotionally and physically safe, free of the need to disconnect.

Chapter 2

Let's Talk About Feelings

"How does that make you feel?"

Our feelings are just feelings—not good or bad in themselves, though they may be pleasant or unpleasant for the person who has them. Feelings are not moral issues. On the other hand, the behaviors we attach to our feelings can easily become moral or even legal issues. We assign a lot of power to feelings, and many of us use feelings as our primary guides for making decisions about our lives.

Many times in my office I've heard a couple talking about divorce because one or both partners no longer "feel happy" in the marriage. And yes, that is our expectation of marriage, and when we lose the *feeling of happiness*, we think that signals it is time to leave. I think it would shock us to know the number of divorces, careers, and wars of this world that have been decided primarily on the basis of feelings.

Sound decision-making has to involve an emotional, feeling component; however, basing a major life decision on feelings alone is as absurd as trying to decide whether to marry or have children strictly on intellectual grounds. It takes both intellectual and emotional components to keep a balance and guide us into the wisest decisions for our lives.

Our culture and unpleasant feelings. Our culture doesn't have much tolerance for unpleasant feelings, especially the Big Three—SAD, MAD, and AFRAID. Within our culture the whole idea of feelings has been greatly misunderstood and mishandled. We are taught to "get rid of" or "get over" any unpleasant feelings, and we are considered "bad" if we have these feelings, or even worse, if we express them. We have been shamed and told we were "bad" for not being able to "get rid of" hurtful feelings.

Most all of us are born with the ability to feel and express a huge range of emotions. Visit any hospital nursery and listen to all the feelings and their expressions. Yet we are barely born before we start getting strong messages from the adults around us to not have the unpleasant feelings. The messages are perceived like this:

Rule Number One: **Don't express what you feel,** because your expression is too loud and urgent, and you aren't the only baby in the nursery. But when we don't know how to hold back expression of what we feel, we have to go on to learn the next rule,

Rule Number Two: **Don't feel your feelings**, which provides some extra protection against expressing them. If you don't feel, you won't express, and you don't get in trouble or hurt as often. And finally we learn,

Rule Number Three: **Don't notice these feelings in yourself, and help others not to notice theirs**. This third rule becomes the guarantee that the child will avoid expressing unpleasant feelings and, thus avoid letting those feelings disturb or upset anyone. This not noticing requires a disconnection between our brains (awareness) and our bodies (stored feelings).

And once we have learned from others and taught ourselves to obey this third unwritten rule, we feel compelled to shut these unpleasant feelings down in others as well as in ourselves, because if we don't, we might actually feel our own unpleasant feelings, or worse still, we might even express some of them!

Numbing ourselves. We have to numb ourselves emotionally in order not to feel or be connected to our feelings. Normally, a person experiences unpleasant feelings off and on throughout the day; if we were taught to "get rid of" or "get over it," however, we will numb ourselves to their very existence within us. In the numbing process, even our *pleasant* feelings get shut down as well. And when that happens, our alive energy and spontaneity disappear. Now we're in the unenviable position of keeping a constant guard on our feelings, censoring ourselves, letting our whole life be governed by the effect expressing our feelings might have on someone else and vice versa.

Then we go on to shame, mock, criticize, or intimidate others who try to express their own unpleasant feelings. We do this for two reasons, first, because we find it too painful to watch someone else express what we have been required to shut down in ourselves, and second, because we are too afraid of what may happen if a lot of unpleasantness comes out. Having been taught practically from the day of our birth to keep the lid on our own unpleasant emotions, as adults many of us back away from other people's sadness, anger, or fear. It's as if letting others feel and express those feelings might open the door for us to acknowledge the same feelings in ourselves, and we can't tolerate the possibility of that.

This learned dynamic of not experiencing or expressing our unpleasant feelings keeps us unfamiliar with these feelings in others and ourselves. We don't even know their names much of the time. We don't know what to do about them, so we just act like they aren't there, or we try to make them go away. Families have practiced these ridiculous rules about feelings for centuries. It's my belief that these rules about not expressing feelings, especially in families, forces us to hold our feelings inside our bodies, thus planting the seeds that eventually sprout into addictions, eating disorders, ADHD, anxiety, OCD and depression, and a host of other psychological and physical ailments.

Feelings may hide, but they don't disappear. We can ignore or hide our feelings, but they don't go away. They are stuffed down and held inside our bodies, and we act them out negatively on others. And in the absence of effective psychotherapy and an education about feelings, most likely we will fail to make the connection between our destructive behaviors and our internal unhappiness.

An unpublished research report (Hulgus, 1992), posits four constants about feelings:

1. Feelings are always present, whether awake or asleep, whether we are aware of them or not.
2. Feelings don't kill. Although the intensity of feelings may make it seem that feelings actually have the power to kill, the reality is they do not now and never will have that much power.
3. Feelings are personal facts, information. It is up to the person having the feelings to communicate them. Whether they are voiced or not, feelings are always communicated. They could be expressed in the form of depression, anxiety, or substance abuse, but however a person decides to communicate, feelings do not disappear.
4. Feelings are nothing more than a report on one's current state of being. By allowing oneself to feel and express feelings, a person is also allowing him or herself to grieve in the most healthy manner possible.

For example, Jane has been unhappy in her marriage for many years, but she can't bring herself to tell her husband Jack how unhappy she is, because she's afraid to upset him or let him know how guilty she feels for not being happy. Jane deals with her dilemma by getting sick often and remaining anxious or depressed. She cries a lot and nags, tries unsuccessfully to control everybody in the family, has "sick headaches" and "nervous spells," or even more serious physical ills that serve as her tickets to a few days in the hospital, where she can get some relief by being cared for by others. She thinks she's hiding her feelings, but you can believe that Jack knows all too well how miserable she is. They just never discuss it, because they both believe that terrible things might happen if they did.

So what does Jack do? Unhappy in the marriage himself, Jack's afraid and ashamed to talk about something so intimate. He can't even acknowledge that he has any unmet emotional needs. So Jack becomes a workaholic, or drinks to excess, or has affairs, or explodes into rages, or finds perfectly good reasons to stay gone from home most of the time. Or maybe he does all of the above.

And then there are Jane and Jack's kids. They too are unhappy, but since the Three Feelings Rules were learned and applied so strictly in their family, they don't feel free to talk about their unhappiness, their anxieties, or their fears.

Mary, the eldest, just tries to be the best, most successful child a family could ever have. She makes all A's, is the captain of the debate team, and gets elected vice-president of her high-school class. She dresses neatly, keeps her room in perfect order, and counts the days until she can move on to college.

Bob, the middle child, hangs out with the wrong crowd, rebels against his parents, starts using alcohol and other drugs, and gets into trouble in and out of school.

And Susie, who is in elementary school, becomes the family clown, spends as much time as possible with her puppy, has trouble concentrating in school and has few friends there, sucks her thumb and sleeps with three teddy bears at night.

None of these three children can let anyone know of the free-floating unhappiness that permeates their home. They just know that they're uncomfortable, not permitted or able to put any specific labels on their feelings or talk about them. This pervasive unhappiness is the big family secret, and they have to help keep it tucked away in silence, while they act out their misery onto themselves and each other. And don't suppose that those same feelings won't go with them into whatever adult relationships they form

Mistaken beliefs about the power of feelings. Our whole society—which includes our homes, schools, churches, workplaces, and leisure pursuits—just is not equipped to handle the SAD, MAD, and AFRAID feelings. No one has taught us how, nor modeled for us what to do with them.

Our warped social education leads us to believe that feelings are bigger than we are, bigger than other people, bigger than life itself! We believe that feelings can destroy or save our lives, make or break our day, give us a good or a bad life. We credit feelings with incredible power.

We even get stuck in the belief that we should never have our feelings hurt, let along hurt the feelings of anyone else! I personally believe that in order to keep growing and learning about ourselves, periodically we all *need* our feelings hurt, if you want to call it that—maybe have someone challenge our behavior is a better way of putting it.

Yet few people will give us the honest feedback we need in a way that we can hear it, so that we can learn about ourselves and grow. Instead of accepting or giving straightforward constructive feedback, most people will walk away, shut down, or back off. "I won't mention it," they'll say. "No need to get things stirred up." Or someone who sees a personal challenge coming will often say, "Oh, just forget it, I'm sorry I ever brought it up."

These beliefs about feelings keep us all at the mercy of our own feelings and the feelings of others. Many of us thus arrive at adulthood taking responsibility for *everyone's* feelings—with complete disregard for our own--living in a type of bondage, afraid to express ourselves, especially if we feel SAD, MAD, or AFRAID.

I believe this thinking has more to do with people becoming addicts than any other beliefs taught in childhood. The very act of learning to hide our feelings creates monumental problems, because we have to hide our true feelings from ourselves as well as others. The result is the cycle of *denial* that all addicts and their families become trapped in (see Chapter 9 on Addictions).

Because they kill our feelings, addictions are considered a *disease of feelings.* Addictions kick in when we need to hide or avoid our real feelings in order to survive. The survival requirements for disconnection and numbness take precedence over the joy of feeling alive, in touch, and being able to express our authentic selves.

Our parents are afraid of their feelings because their parents were afraid of theirs and their parents were afraid of theirs, etc., and they taught us the same fears. Thus because none of us feels free to express our own genuine inner self, disconnection from our own vital inner awareness begins.

Unpleasant feelings have a valuable purpose. Nature had a specific purpose in giving us those unpleasant feelings. If we could recognize unpleasant feelings as assets, instead of believing that having them means something's "wrong" or "inferior" about us, we could use them as they were designed to be used—primarily to let us know that we are unhappy, afraid, or uncomfortable with some circumstance in our life. Unpleasant feelings are there to aid our survival, to give us guidance or indications throughout each day, hour, and minute, supporting better judgments about our lives and interactions with others. Learning to handle our unpleasant feelings helps us stretch into the personal growth that develops our more mature life skills.

When we disconnect ourselves from these feelings, we impair our natural ability to judge a situation or a person as safe or unsafe, conducive to our well-being or destructive to it. Those who teach us not to trust our feelings, especially the unpleasant ones, cut us off from a vital information source that often involves our personal safety. We find it hard to trust and be truly close to *anyone*, because we haven't been allowed to know or develop our own judgment. In terms of both safety and trust, this becomes a far too costly way to live, when other options exist.

As Julie approached puberty, her mother's brother began to look for opportunities to be with her in a room when no one else was there. He would touch her in inappropriate ways, then tell her that if she told, he would make her sorry or call her a liar. Julie feared and hated these encounters, yet she couldn't haul off and punch her uncle, because he would tell on her, and she would surely be punished for that. Nor did she tell her mom what he was doing, because she felt sure her mom would just say, "Don't be ridiculous! You know Uncle Sid loves you and means well. He would never hurt you!"

So Julie was trapped. Her uncle was the perpetrator, yet Julie ended up feeling guilty and blaming herself, as if she had somehow brought this on herself and was a contributor to the unhealthy situation. Every time she recalled the bad feelings she had about her uncle she felt ashamed, because children are supposed to love their uncles. Fortunately, she did pay attention to her feelings at least to the extent of devising an avoidance strategy, making sure never to let herself get caught off-guard with Uncle Sid in a room alone, so that he couldn't continue the molestation. But Julie had difficulty trusting familiar, supposedly "nice" people as a result, and it affected her adult relationships.

This is only one example of how such things happen in families. Reports continue to surface in the media of inappropriate behavior on the part of supposedly trustworthy adults—church youth workers, pastors, teachers, even school principals and bosses. Such things happen at school, work, church, and in relationships every day.

Frances, an abused wife, is wretched in her battered life, yet her financially successful husband Fred tells her after every tirade how much he loves her and threatens her if she tries to leave him. So Frances stuffs her fear, her sadness, and her anger deep down inside and rationalizes her plight by telling herself, "But he loves me and he needs me! I can't leave him, because I can't support myself, and anyway, if I did, he might really hurt me."

Frances's unpleasant feelings were put there at birth for her protection, yet in her upbringing she learned not to feel these feelings, much less express them boldly or courageously. And in the end Frances's inability to express her feelings appropriately may even cost her her life, not to mention the unhealthy, self-destructive behavior she is modeling for her children.

Disconnection turns feelings into harmful actions. Because our culture allows and encourages us to experience the happy, positive feelings in life those feelings are indeed experienced and expressed. Our society enjoys our happy, pleasant feelings with us. When we are experiencing happiness, people enjoy it with us by laughing, playing, and communicating with us about it. On the other hand, because we're taught to keep unpleasant feelings to ourselves, the only way to be sure we won't upset anyone with our feelings is to let out only the pleasant ones, keeping the rest hidden so deeply that we don't even know they are there.

Where the damage happens. We disconnect ourselves from our unpleasant feelings, walk around with them stuffed down inside our body, and then proceed to *act them out* on everyone else! Even worse, we don't even know that we're doing it. We learn to "stuff" our own unwanted feelings and to ignore, dismiss, criticize, blame, shame, attack, or avoid people who try to express unpleasant feelings of their own. With these powerful feelings stored inside our bodies, we can keep from knowing and naming our feelings only by disconnecting our heads from our bodies, so that's exactly what we do. No matter how many warning messages our bodies send, our brain simply ignores them, at least until the pain becomes unbearable, and then we either seek help or make the ultimate disconnect—opt out of life.

Then, too, we believe that the unpleasant feelings others have will rub off onto us, if we address them or help someone deal with them. In his excellent book *Raising An Emotionally Intelligent Child*, John Gottman says of parents who ignore or try to shut down unpleasant feelings in their children,

> Parents who dismiss their kids' pain view unpleasant feelings like weeds, to address those feelings is like watering and fertilizing weeds. Talking about unpleasant feelings makes them grow, and they will eventually just take over your lives. It's better to just "get rid" of them, then they can't hurt you.

This may sound like juvenile thinking and behavior, but we do in fact behave in immature, childlike ways when we are faced with unpleasant feelings, simply because no one has taught us what else to do with them. Probably at one time in our history human beings couldn't afford to look at or address unpleasantness, because they were so preoccupied with surviving. Anything unpleasant was taken care of swiftly and drastically with a fight, a club, a knife, or a gun, moving to another settlement—whatever would get things back to normal quickly, so people could get refocused on survival.

Understanding feelings and learning new life skills. Fortunately for us today we have the time to deal with feelings productively—if we will take it. And if our lives are ever to become better, it's essential that we begin, or we'll continue to make the same miserable mistakes over and over again, continuing to do the same things we've always done and expecting different results. Finding a better life means mastering new life skills, and learning to recognize and express our feelings appropriately is one of those most valuable skills.

What are we teaching our kids about feelings? *Kids attach importance to whatever they have seen their parents attend to in themselves and in others.* So kids become ashamed and embarrassed about asking for help or even acknowledging that they are SAD, MAD, or AFRAID, when they have seen their parents avoid these feelings themselves. When children experience adults as attending more to outer needs (physical) than inner needs (emotional), they interpret the lack of attention to unpleasant feelings as a signal that people *shouldn't have* feelings of that sort.

When we either stuff down or avoid expressions of negative feelings in ourselves, we're teaching our kids to ignore those feelings. They see us deny or "get rid of" or "get over" unpleasant feelings, rather than see us experience, name, and work to express them in productive ways.

I'm tempted to put this next paragraph in all capital letters, because that's how important it is. *Kids need to hear their parents disagree, see them cry (not hysterically), watch them address anger (not rage), and observe them as they work through their differences appropriately. And all adults, whether parents or not, need to learn to work through their differences appropriately in order to live an emotionally healthy life.*

Nothing is sadder than someone who's been taught to stuff or hide real feelings, then moves on to manipulate and attempt to control others, use chemicals to cope with life, escape from the home situation, overwork, or stay "busy," shop, eat, zone out, or stay "sick," depressed, or anxious most of the time.

Adults use addictions to *act out their deeply hidden feelings*, instead of acknowledging them, talking about them, and working through them with each other and within themselves. And when children see adults do it that way, they conclude that those are the *normal* methods, which they must adopt themselves.

No one controls another's feelings. We cannot control other peoples' feelings, even though we believe we can. We don't have that kind of power—to decide what someone will or will not feel, to decide whether someone's feelings will or will not be hurt. We don't get to assign feelings to ourselves, or to other people. If we had that power, we would assign ourselves and everybody else to be happy all of the time!

We come to believe we have the power to decide others' feelings because we are given that message by our parents, usually daily, as children: *"You make me so happy* when you make those good grades," or *"You make me so mad* when you act that way." Even though we don't have such power now and never did, what we did have was powerful— those godlike people in our lives telling us we could make or break their day, even make or break their *lives.* I say godlike, because a child believes his or her very survival depends upon those same caregivers.

These are powerful messages to give a child, and the child will take them in as true, because those messages are coming from godlike people, and children don't even realize that they can believe and act otherwise. Neither do many adults, in fact, until the pain becomes intolerable. So, children learn, by virtue of being told repeatedly, that they can manipulate and control others' feelings. No wonder children feel so responsible for all the good and bad things that happen in their lives. If Mom and Dad get a divorce, it must be Jill's fault, no matter how many times her mom and her dad tell her it isn't so. The parents have already taught Jill that she's responsible for everyone's happiness, sadness, anger, grief, etc. And she believes it.

Often we hear people say, "I don't want to tell Mary that, because it would hurt her feelings." In therapy, when I ask one or the other partner to tell the spouse how he or she really feels about the relationship, more often than not that partner will say, "Saundra, I couldn't do that, because it might really hurt his or her feelings."

So then I ask the listening partner, "Which would you rather have, hurt feelings, or a divorce?" As you can imagine, the answer 100% of the time is, "Hurt feelings, any day of the week!"

Understanding our limits. Our inability to control another's feelings does not, however, give us license to express ourselves in any way we choose. Words and behaviors have consequences, and mature people expect to live with the consequences of their words and deeds. So now we get into *boundary issues.* In a partnering relationship, each person is responsible for telling the other when hurt arises from something that is said or done. We owe each other this accountability for our behavior.

One partner in a relationship never bears the full burden of making that relationship work or keeping the other partner happy. We can *try* to make someone happy, even give up our own wants and needs to make him or her happy, but in the end it's the individual's decision whether to be happy or not. *We cannot make anyone happy. Being happy is an individual choice.*

"But what if he gets mad?" Well, what if he does? Anger works the same way. We can get in someone's face and try to make him or her angry, but again, that person decides whether or not to get angry. Often, we may try extra-hard not to upset someone, but the person gets angry anyway. Or we could be dealing with an undiagnosed *depression* in a person who *seems* angry, when that perceived anger is actually a cover-up for depression or fear. In our society men are given more permission to be angry than to be depressed, so we see more angry men. On the other hand, because we teach our girls it isn't "nice" to be angry, women tend to cover their anger with sadness or fear, so we see more depressed, anxious women.

Each of us has the final say in how we feel and what we do about it. We all know people in relationships where one partner seems to sacrifice his or her life to make the other partner happy, yet it doesn't work. That's because the person who's trying so hard lacks ultimate control over the other person's feelings. In fact, the person being catered to may actually come to scorn or disdain the sacrificing one: "Who, her? Forget her. She doesn't know what she wants. She'll do whatever I say."

David, a CPA, has to drive 20 miles on the interstate to and from work every day. Suppose a young man in a snappy red sports car driving 90 miles an hour in a 65-mile zone changes lanes abruptly, without signaling, and cuts in front of David, almost causing him to wreck. The speeder may have set out intentionally to antagonize David, because he thinks David's driving too conservatively, or he may just be reckless. But no matter what his intentions are, David is the one who decides whether to indulge in road-rage and seek to run the guy off the road, or whether to take his foot off the gas, ease over a lane, and let the speeder go on at his own risk.

Imagine what this world would be like if we'd been taught that it is not only appropriate but necessary to express what we truly feel. Imagine how many different ways we could have developed to express ourselves appropriately. Instead, we learn to hide our real feelings, then act them out on other people. Just imagine the degree of honesty we could operate from, being able to be genuine with ourselves and others. We could be congruent—our words would match our actions, our outsides would match our insides. When a person is able to arrive at that state, he or she is beginning to become a whole, healthy individual.

When you think about it, genuine connected people who are in touch with their feelings and know appropriate ways to express them are actually a thousand times less hurtful than people who lack these qualities and stay numbed-out to their true feelings.

Remember, feelings are not the problem. How we choose to express our feelings becomes the problem.

The relationship disabler. There's no question that the person who withholds all outward expression of feelings causes the most serious damage in relationships. Such a person is choosing to avoid becoming intimate or vulnerable with another, ruling out a genuinely connected relationship. Dealing with such a person is as frustrating as trying to connect emotionally with an empty chair. He or she avoids any emotional risk by holding feelings inside, not giving others even a clue of what is really going on with them. Of course eventually, the volcano explodes, or the resentment river overflows, when the Quiet One *acts out* all of his or her stored unpleasant feelings onto others.

Such a person is like the proverbial bull in the china closet, doing horrendous damage, yet unaware that any harm is being done. Often such a person is actually shocked that anything he or she has said or done might upset someone else.

"I can't believe you said that (or did that)!" the hurt partner may wail.

"Did what? Said what?" the Quiet One responds. "*You're* the one causing all the ruckus!"

This seemingly quiet, calm person is *the most toxic of all,* even though he or she may, through silence and lack of expression, impress us initially as the strongest one of the lot, the one who appears to "have it all together." In relationships, there's no substitute for honesty, openness, and willingness when it comes to expressing feelings.

Trying to "fix" people's feelings doesn't work. Feelings need a special kind of attention, but they do not need to be "fixed." In fact, they can't be. They are just there with us and come upon us. In many cases, particularly very stressful situations, we cannot predict what our feelings will be. We cannot decide which feelings are going to come upon us before they arrive. If we could, we would all choose only happy feelings, no matter what, but our systems don't work that way.

Feelings are not moral issues; however, the behaviors we attach to our feelings may become moral issues. We don't choose the feelings, but we certainly choose the behaviors that attach to our feelings. Suppose I'm angry with my friend Debra, and I tell you about it. Then suppose you say, "But, Saundra, you shouldn't be mad at Debra! She is really a nice person."

(1) Am I still mad at Debra?
(2) Am I now also mad at you for negating my feelings and shaming me for having them?

The answer to both questions is YES!

So now I am twice as mad, because I was mad to begin with, then you tried to shame me out of my real feelings. So, you see, in trying to "help" me and "fix" my unpleasant feelings, you have actually made matters twice as bad.

What we can do to help. What would have helped me in this situation? I needed someone to *listen to me* and *validate my feelings unconditionally.* Exactly what does that mean, the unconditional validation of one's feelings?

Validation means that I allow you to express whatever feelings you have without judging, moralizing, rationalizing, giving my opinion, editing, or adding my two cents' worth. Whatever your reality is, I make room for it in our relationship, right here, right now.

Unconditional validation is about *allowing each other to be different.* It sends the message that you do not have to see the world through my eyes. Our relationship has space for your world as well as mine. Validation does not mean I agree with the feelings you have, or that I justify them or even understand how you could feel that way. I just acknowledge that this is the way it is for you, right now.

Neither does validation mean that I approve of the behavior you've chosen to attach to your feelings. Your behavior may even be so inappropriate that I feel a need to intervene by restraining you or calling for some outside help. Fortunately, this is rarely the case.

In any relationship, what all of us need and long for is to be *heard* and *validated* as a valuable person with both pleasant and unpleasant feelings throughout each and every day. If we could learn this in a genuine way, we could give up our anxiety about unpleasant feelings and deal with them, instead of acting them out on others as well as ourselves.

Intent is not the issue. During a time when my husband was learning this dynamic about feelings, he and I were at the mall when he overheard one woman say to another, "She can't be upset, because I know what I said, and I *wasn't trying* to upset her!"

My husband, impressed, said to me, "Now, that's a perfect example of one person trying to assign another person particular feelings—feelings she thought the other woman *should be having*, because of her *own* intent."

Exactly right. Our intent has absolutely no bearing on how someone will take in and experience what we say or do. In healthy relationships, we realize this and accept that we still say and do things that may evoke hurt in other people, even though we didn't intend that result. Owning this is a very grown-up skill. It is a difficult dynamic for any of us to own and probably the most difficult feedback we have to hear from our partners. I can remember going out of my way trying to *not hurt* someone, only to have it end with that person feeling more hurt than if I had done nothing.

How we try to dance around the feelings of others. Just listen to the way we talk, when fear of others' feelings drives us to try to manipulate their feelings. We might say, "Now, don't get mad, but . . . " or "You're probably going to be mad at me, but . . . " or "Promise you won't be mad at me, but . . . " Going at it this way, we're hoping to continue feeling safe in the relationship by attempting to control the other person's feelings.

Instead of trying to control how a person feels, which is impossible anyway, isn't it more effective to say, "*When* you get mad at me [which you most certainly will if we try to have a connected relationship], here is how I would like you to handle your anger with me_____?" (You fill in the blank.) In other words, be realistic and specific.

Learning this dynamic and working with it. We all have very different realities because of our varying histories, and those differences make our relationships challenging and sometimes tedious. In order to have healthy relationships, we need to know our partner's history and accept our differences, so that we can give up the urgent need to *change* him or her. We can succeed in our relationships, if we have people in our lives who will work with us and allow us to work with them on this dynamic, which is about learning to harmonize our histories rather than fight because of them. Partners who want their partnership to endure must take this dynamic seriously and work with each other on it. I believe that most misunderstandings between partners begin somewhere along this path of differentiation.

Suppose Linda tells her husband Larry when he comes in from work, "Hurry up and put your jeans on, because we're headed for the block barbecue." Now, right away Larry is in a dilemma. He doesn't want to hurt her feelings, nor does he want to go. So, with the best intent in the world, he says, "Honey, I didn't know anything about a party this evening, and I'm really tired. How would you feel if I didn't go?"

Was that what Linda wanted to hear? Of course not. She bursts into tears and wails, "You don't love me any more!"

At this point, Larry has a choice to make. If he gives in and goes, allowing his tiredness and resistance to be completely negated because Linda got so upset, he will resent his choice—*a victim, childlike decision.* His anger will ooze out of him anyway, regardless of how hard he tries to hold it in.

Or he can force his will on Linda and say, "I'm not going, because I don't want to, and that's that. Cry all you want to, but I'm not changing my mind!"—*an angry, parental decision.*

Or he can ask Linda to talk with him for a few minutes about their dilemma. He can ask her to fully hear his feelings around this issue, then listen to her feelings about it, then arrive at a decision together that will somehow work for both of them—*a healthy partnering decision.*

Making a *partnering* decision doesn't mean either partner ends up getting his or her way absolutely. A partnering decision means both partners are included in the process and have agreed upon whatever decision is reached. Both partners share the power of expressing their genuine reality about the problem, discussing any angles that need to be heard by the other, and arriving at a workable solution for both. It's unrealistic to think that we won't ever get upset with our mate or our kids or anyone else with whom we want to be close. And it's equally unrealistic to think we won't ever upset them. We will upset them, and they will upset us, too, at some point. People trying to connect and be close to each other often upset each other. When two *alive* beings try to connect, sparks result, just as when two wires carrying a live current of electricity touch.

Now, if one of those two wires or one of those two human beings becomes "dead"—not flowing with *alive* energy—there are no sparks. Frequently, when a relationship becomes painful—no longer feels emotionally safe—

either or both partners go numb and stop the flow of their *alive* energy. Rather than being a signal to give up on the relationship, this emotional deadness is actually the signal to go to work to improve it.

How important are feelings? I believe we can change our lives drastically for the better by learning to manage the energy of our feelings so that we can use our feelings in the constructive way they were originally designed to be used. We were taught to fear our unpleasant feelings, and we've taught our kids to do the same. They have watched us as we killed off any feelings we feared. Our kids have the availability of much more toxic methods of killing their feelings. Our challenge as adults is to *get familiar with these unpleasant feelings*, especially the Big Three--SAD, MAD, AFRAID—and *teach our children to master the management of these feelings* in order to take advantage of the power they can provide for their lives.

Chapter 3

Learning to Handle Anger

"I can't believe you got mad over a little thing like that!"

As human beings, we come wired with the ability to feel a huge range of inborn emotions. Some of these emotions we experience as pleasant, others we experience as unpleasant. Anger seems to be the most misunderstood and has taken the worst rap of all. For that reason, I invite you to help me take anger out of the closet, understand what it's really about, and try to operate from a more enlightened perspective in regard to it.

Most of us have been taught since childhood that "You shouldn't get angry," or "It isn't nice to get angry," or "If you get angry, bad things will happen."

As a therapist, I don't see it that way. I believe strongly that anger has a higher purpose than to just upset us or hurt us. If we don't get angry, or if we aren't connected enough with our anger to allow ourselves to feel it, our emotional and physical survival will be difficult or even impossible in the long run.

It may surprise you to know that every one of us gets angry several times every day, yet I've heard countless people say, and really believe, "I never really get angry." Someone who denies ever being angry has forced a disconnection between their brain (awareness) and their body (where feelings are stored) that keeps them unaware of their feelings.

When that disconnect happens, we become convinced that those highly charged angry feelings do not even exist. Oh, but they do! They're still alive and at work in our bodies, even though we may disconnect our awareness from them out of a conscious or unconscious belief that our survival requires it.

One of the most memorable Power Struggles I've ever worked with in my practice had persisted for 45 years. The couple came in eager to tell me, "We've never had a fuss in all our forty-five years together." Of course, the marriage was dead. They had killed off the energy of their relationship in order to survive it. They lived in the same house, but on two separate emotional islands. These two seasoned troupers seemed to view the absence of challenge and confrontation in their relationship as a positive feature, because their families of origin had taught them never to feel or address their anger. What could they do, then, but deny that it was ever there? Most of us have been taught the same way.

Of course the anger is there, stored in our bodies! *If anger isn't acknowledged or allowed expression in an honest, direct, open way, it will ooze out of us in an indirect, dishonest, destructive way.* When a person refuses to acknowledge or express anger constructively, everyone who tries to be close to that person will feel it consciously and unconsciously, yet no one is allowed to put a name to it or talk about it. Living with unacknowledged anger is the emotional equivalent of sitting on a rumbling volcano, or a powder keg with the fuse lit.

Not feeling anger, not addressing it, denying that it exists—these methods of dealing or not dealing with anger didn't spring up overnight. Our parents were taught these self-defeating ways of managing anger by their parents, and their parents were taught the same thing by their parents, so that generation after generation passed these avoidant techniques down to us. And many of us have, sadly, passed down these same detrimental methods to our kids. At some point, the cycle must stop so we can appreciate and use anger the way it was originally designed to work for us, instead of viewing anger as a character flaw.

Our expressions of anger. In our society, anger is normally expressed as rage, silence, or both. I use the word "normally" because most of us actually believe the normal way of being angry is either to go into a rage or to avoid through silence. This is how most of us saw anger modeled by adults when we were growing up. As impressionable young children, we saw anger used as a weapon to hurt others, or keep others feeling unsafe.

Yet rage and silence are not about being angry. These inappropriate defense mechanisms to anger are about *avoiding, facing up to the real problems*—thus inadvertently creating even more injury. Rage and silence are about manipulating others because of feelings we don't know how to, or will not, directly address.

The difference in anger and rage. *Anger is target-specific* and does not engulf the whole universe. Anger is the warning light signaling, "Something here isn't going the way that's comfortable for me." On the other hand, *rage is global*, striking out in all directions at everything, while avoiding the specific problem. The fear that many of us harbor about the damage anger can do actually arises from the damage we have seen created by rage. Rage is anger gone wild, like a double-barreled shotgun spewing buckshot in every direction.

Suppose your partner doesn't believe that he rages or even has a bad temper. Then you must decide what your own bottom line is and set your boundaries accordingly. If you have children, do you want your children exposed to this terrifying and seemingly out-of-control behavior? The children of ragers grow up to be ragers or silent withdrawers, unless they can be shown a better way. Steps will need to be taken to inform and help the rager get the education, skills, and counseling necessary to stop the tirades. Allowing this inappropriate, scary behavior to continue does not help the rager, and it surely damages the family.

You are never doing anyone a favor by allowing intolerable behavior to continue. This sentence always makes me think of my dad. We were all so afraid of him and his temper, and out of our own fear, we protected his intolerable behavior. I can see now that we did not do him a favor. Before he died at age 84, there was not one person left on this earth who cared one thing about him. He had forcefully driven away his family and anyone who could have cared about him. I wish we had confronted him and given him the opportunity to hear how we experienced him. Maybe that could have made a difference for him and our family.

One word of caution. Further along in the chapter I write about planning for and practice at managing anger, but be aware that people who habitually allow their anger to go on to rage will usually resist such planning and practice. Why? Because in situations that evoke their anger, they're used to just letting it all fly against the wall. *They get high on raging.* Ragers do not like to be interrupted, and this format is an interruption. Be patient, without insisting that they *enjoy* this new way of handling anger. They don't need to enjoy it or even agree with it. All you're asking is that they be willing to try it as a new idea with a proven track record that will help both partners get to a safer place in the relationship. *Building this new belief system* about anger and your relationship will take lots of rehearsals and practice runs, so give yourselves time to learn.

The positive energy of anger We've all seen the negativity of people getting upset with each other. Most of us, however, have never witnessed anger as a *positive* experience, with everybody learning a better way to operate with each other, a better way to live.

When partners ignore or shut down their anger, they are shutting down a vital energy in their relationship. Anger is a passionate energy driven by adrenaline, a secretion of our endocrine glands that helps us stand up for and protect ourselves. Sexual intimacy is another passionate energy, driven by the brain chemicals called endorphins, which allow us to experience the euphoria of an affectionate physical connection.

Both of these body chemicals—adrenaline and endorphins—are aggressive, action-directed hormones. Shutting down the energy of these action hormones kills the *aliveness* of the relationship and replaces it with numbness, which eventually progresses to the point that the relationship feels dead. When we give up our angry energy, we also give up the passion, because both are *alive* energies. Somehow, we come to believe that *any* form of highly charged emotional energy is "bad," because we have experienced the misuse of it in relationships.

Anger has a positive purpose. Emotions are neither bad nor good. Emotions just *are*, given to us to enrich and safeguard our life. Anger is only a signal to us that we are not liking something. Anger is like a light that comes on to let us know we're feeling uncomfortable or unhappy, or experiencing something unpleasant. It's like a car's warning light, or a message on our computer screen, or crossing lights that flash when a train is coming through. We appreciate those lights. We rely on those signals, and we want them working all the time. In fact, if one of them fails to alert us even once, we're quick to have it fixed.

On the other hand, when our emotional system tries to alert us, through anger, that we need to attend to something, instead of heeding the warning and dealing with its cause, we tend to stuff, ignore, minimize, rationalize, let someone talk us out of our awareness of the feeling, and disconnect ourselves from that signal as quickly as possible. *We're still angry, but depriving ourselves of the knowledge or vital information our anger could have given us.*

If we were to handle our anger warning appropriately, we would take some action or follow some course directed toward resolution around whatever or whoever is presenting the discomfort. Bringing the problem into the light of day and dealing with it in emotional honesty is a learnable life skill that can benefit us all. Learning that skill is one of the essential tasks of becoming a grown-up, emotionally healthy person.

Passivity doesn't work. People who handle anger passively become doormats, and what happens to doormats? People walk all over them, and eventually they wear out and get thrown out. If we choose to deal with our anger passively we may do it in a number of ways:

- "Stuff" it inside, pretending it isn't there, do nothing.
- Minimize it — "Oh, it's nothing, really."
- Rationalize and intellectualize — "Well, you can't blame him. He was abused as a child.
- Justify another's unfair behavior — "It's my fault, I shouldn't have said anything."

- Deny that we're angry when confronted — "Oh, no, I'm not angry.
  I just overreacted, but now everything's fine."

When taking a passive approach, our anger will then be "acted out" onto others in hurtful ways that do not seem associated with our anger. Acting out anger is a Victim's way of avoiding responsibility for taking care of himself or herself. Victims act out their anger by sulking, withdrawing, silence, being busy, sick, unavailable, pitiful, drinking, drugging, having affairs, slamming doors and drawers.

People who act out their anger passively will *forget* to meet some responsibility another person expects them to carry out, for example, or will be chronically *late* for meetings with that person. If the other person tries to address that behavior, the acting- out person may say, "What are you talking about? I don't understand."

Another example of acting out anger is *displacing it* onto another target. The classic scenario here is the boss who chews out Dad. Dad goes home and fusses at Mom. Mom fusses at child, child kicks the dog, dog bites the cat, cat eats the goldfish. Everyone in this sequence moved down the ladder to express their anger. No one who was responsible for the misplaced angry behavior got addressed, so no one was required to be accountable for any inappropriateness. Long lists could be made of the results of the passive approach, none of them productive.

Aggression doesn't work either. If we handle our anger in an aggressive way, we have another long list to choose from. We may yell, berate, blame, name-call, shame, throw or smash things, or use physical force in some other way. In other words, if we choose to address our anger aggressively, we will *attack* the other person either verbally or physically.

With this approach, no matter what form the aggressive or rageful outburst may take, neither the anger nor its cause will ever be addressed in a way that leads to resolution. On the contrary, the outcome may be a venting, ranting, raging session about everything that has upset the aggressively angry person over the last twenty years.

If anger is there, we can learn to feel and manage it. We can learn many appropriate ways of handling our anger, but *we cannot make ourselves not get angry.* We can, however, keep ourselves completely numbed-out to our anger, so that we don't have to feel or address it. And numbing ourselves out to our anger requires the help of addictive behaviors, such as using alcohol, drugs, work, sex, food, etc. When we numb ourselves out so that we don't feel the anger, we either shut down our natural potential for the feel-good emotions, or, alternatively, produce a temporary euphoria by whatever it is that we use to get high, but as that temporary euphoria wears off, we're right back where we started—numb.

This numbness creates enormous internal stress in our bodies, our lives, and relationships, because our relationships will feel dead. The dead feeling will often manifest in depression, or in some people, be experienced as anxiety or even panic from having to *give up the aliveness* in their primary relationships.

Many partners of alcoholics or addicts have used this numbing-out response as a way of trying to survive in the relationship—essentially a Victim stance. The addict engages in behaviors that would evoke anger in a balanced, mature partner, but because most partners of addicts lack useful anger-management skills and fear being abused, raged at, or abandoned, the partner may numb out and choose to suffer in silence, even ignoring the fact that suffering is taking place. The common result is depression plus a host of other physical and psychological ills.

When we adults get uncomfortable in relationships, our reactions often run the gamut from avoidance of *any* conflict to aggressive confrontation of *every* problem. Until we learn better coping skills, some of us disconnect by running away, while others freeze into submission, or fight it out then and there, or space out and dissociate. This is the fight-or-flight syndrome, coming from the most primitive part of our survival brain—the Reptilian Brain. This basic survival part of us kicks in unconsciously to protect us, and it is reactive, like a knee jerk. Such reactions lead to disconnection from our partners and sabotage any workable resolution within the relationship.

Staying connected—the road to resolution. We have a difficult time recognizing that staying connected during conflict can be a positive, even an essential process. Most of us have had little if any practice in the process of working toward some form of resolution both partners can agree upon, a resolution that will allow us to stretch into the new growth we need in order to become healthy partners.

This staying-connected-for-resolution process requires several skills, using the Intentional Dialogue process, we can:

- Talk honestly about our experience, our reality (using more than four sentences)
- Be open to new ideas, the other partner's view and reality

- Go back over possibilities for resolution that haven't worked in the past and discover why, and,
- Most important, listen to the context/circumstances that surrounds the other partner's reality in order to hear their pain and relate with genuine empathy.

How anger can catch us off guard. We may at times disappoint and do things that our partner interprets as threatening, without meaning to or even knowing it, until we experience the partner's response of anger. This is often bewildering and unbelievable to us, since we had no *intention* of upsetting anyone.

Such reactions will be less likely to catch us unprepared if we begin with the reality that we often upset others *unintentionally*, and vice versa. Others often upset us too, regardless of whether that was their intent. We're not all "coming from the same place." Your life experience is different from mine, and what may seem perfectly reasonable to me may feel to you like a personal attack. So the best approach is to go into relationships prepared with this understanding. Every one of us is unique, with a unique set of emotional experiences. My relationship history isn't the same as your relationship history. These differences are reality, ever present in daily life with other people, especially our partners and families.

Lay the groundwork before anger comes. Anger will come in any relationship where an *alive* connection is trying to happen. So instead of saying, "I hope this doesn't make you mad at me, but . . ." a more realistic approach is learning to say, "When my behaviors or words upset you, I prefer that you handle your anger with me by . . ."

Instruct the other person how you want to be informed when you've done something to arouse their anger. *Do this instructing before anyone is upset.* Most of us get this information in a heated moment and in such a hurtful way that we can't hear it or take it in at the time. By then the damage is usually done. Both partners are in their defensive modes, and they're off to the races.

When you instruct, explain what would help you feel safe with that person, even though he or she is angry with you. For example, you might say, "I would appreciate it if you hold your volume down, keep your facial expressions as soft as possible, speak respectfully to me and about me, stay focused on my behaviors and not on my character as a person," and specify whatever else would help you to stay connected and hear what you have done to upset the person, as well as how you can make it right.

Whenever someone who's angry at you vents on you without including this last piece—how you can make things right—all they have done is vent, and you deserve more. *Do not allow venting.* Make a steadfast rule: "I'm willing to hear your anger, if at the same time you suggest things I can do or say that would feel better to you than the things I'm presently doing or saying that upset you."

What to do when the ground rules are being ignored. It's also important, in advance of any angry conflict, to set a plan with that particular person about what you will do if he or she does not honor your stated requests for telling you about their anger.

For example, you might ask if the other person would allow you to *supply a gentle cue about volume:* "Could you please lower your voice?"

Or maybe you could agree *that you will both take a pause, gently leave the room (no slamming doors!), and come back within an agreed-upon time to try again.*

It is crucial to rehearse this scenario before you need it. You both need to agree upon the approach you'll take and be willing to cooperate with the outcome. Although it may seem too rehearsed, you actually need to *script* and *choreograph* your anger scene ahead of time. Otherwise, you'll continue the familiar dance and face the usual emotional disaster with hurt feelings, sulking, and subsequent isolation.

When partners are willing to let it, anger can serve as the biggest area of growth for the relationship and thus the best potential vehicle for partners to reach a deeper, more connected level. As you work together to learn to manage anger constructively, you will gain respect for each other and invest more emotional energy in your relationship. Most importantly, you will be *building the belief system* that says, *We can learn to manage our angry energy within the relationship, rather than allowing the anger to dominate and wreck it.*

As couples learn to manage their angry energy and discover what that energy is really trying to teach them, their kids will soak up these tools also and won't feel defeated by their own anger. Sally is 34, has two kids ages 6 and 4 with her husband, Sam, and has just started back to college to finish her degree in accounting. Sam is pleased she's going back to school and looks forward to her future ability to help with the family expenses. His own job takes up most of his time, however, so that he isn't home to pick up the slack for her. They have come to therapy because Sally is unhappy about "Sam's lack of involvement with their children." She is critical of his attempts, considers them half-hearted, and tells Sam so. Sam feels like no matter what he does, it is "never enough" and he can "never please Sally."

This couple is stuck in a hidden agenda. What the two of them are stating as the "presenting problem" isn't what is really going on. Because neither partner has learned to look beneath their anger to find the real source of their pain, they argue, fuss, distance, and go about their separate lives, with little else but their two children holding their partnership together.

As we unraveled the threads of their discontent, we discovered how their present-day anger had mixed automatically and unconsciously with old stored anger from their childhoods (see Chapter 1 for more on unresolved childhood issues). So, whatever makes us angry today is intensified by material stored in our unconscious and never been dealt with. The present-day anger matches up to another angry feeling and situational holdover from the past that lies dormant until our partner awakens that old unresolved pain.

Sally and Sam had never examined their histories around anger and how they had seen anger played out in their childhood. As we began to examine their histories, we found that because Sam was the youngest of four, as a child no one had ever spent much time with him. Other than being considered cute and funny, he didn't perceive that he had much impact on his family. Nothing he did really got their attention, so he spent his childhood either with friends or entertaining himself. Sam rarely expressed any anger as a child, because his father and one older brother, who both had temper tantrums and raged, expressed so much anger that little Sam felt terrified and overwhelmed.

Sally, on the other hand, was the second daughter who lived in the shadow of her older, near-perfect sister. Sally tried hard to achieve and shine with her family; however, she felt they expected her to take care of herself without much help from them. They were all on their separate paths. Her dad was usually away at work, and her mom was sickly and had to stay in bed most days. Sally learned to take care of many responsibilities, including her baby brother, without asking for or expecting anyone else's involvement. No one in Sally's family, except the young brother, expressed any anger, and Sally's parents both avoided conflict and unpleasantness, especially around feelings.

As kids growing up, both Sally and Sam were fairly content, but each learned to avoid any awareness that they harbored anger about their respective families' lack of involvement in their lives. They accepted this way of growing up as *normal* and felt guilty and embarrassed to even admit that they were unhappy about parts of their childhood.

As this couple began to open up and talk about their real feelings, we discovered that Sally was really angry about the lack of attention Sam was showing *her*. His distance was sending her the same hurtful message she got in childhood: "You're on your own. Take care of things, don't need me." As her unconscious was picking up on this message—a message of which Sally was unaware, because *it was unconscious*— she began feeling bewildered and too vulnerable to tell him how his behavior was hurting her, instead she started criticizing Sam about his dealings with the children.

Sam had felt defeated in their relationship, too, but did not see that he was entitled to his anger around Sally's criticisms of him as a father. Sam began opening up and discovering his anger at a conscious level, and his right to express his anger at Sally. His job was to work with Sally and teach her how she could tell him about her discontent in a nonjudgmental way, so that he could take it in without withdrawing to defend himself and survive.

As both Sam and Sally learned to stay present with each other, hear their different realities, and set aside their defenses to state what each needed from the other, they began to work through their issues and *build the belief system* that they could stay connected while having conflict. Also, as each began to understand the wounding that the defenses had been covering up, they were able to soften those defenses and listen with empathy to their partner.

Discovering the link between today's wounding and the wounding that took place in childhood is vital. Partners need to begin to picture a hurting child rather than an angry adult, and in order to understand how each partner must be feeling today, they need to be able to feel how that child must have felt back then. This connection between the child within and the surviving adult allows the partner to see the vulnerability that the adult carries and hides with defenses. One would hope that none of us would be as eager to attack a wounded child as we would an angry adult. Usually when we can see the vulnerability of our partner, our heart softens, and genuine empathy enters the relationship. Empathy is what creates the connection.

Why we hesitate to say what we need. The format I've proposed requires people to be willing to be *vulnerable* with each other, *take the risk* of letting the other know what would help him or her feel safe. Most of us feel vulnerable when we reveal what we really want and need in our relationship, because as kids we may have been teased, made fun of, criticized, and shamed for even having needs, let alone speaking them out loud. We may have been told it's "wrong" and "selfish" to suggest to anyone else how we want to be handled, or even to suggest that we have emotional needs.

We learned to endure, not to speak up. We saw our parents endure and avoid the working through and resolution of angry issues in ways that would have worked for both partners. We saw them hurt each other repeatedly, and many times a divorce was the result of how a couple dealt with each other and their marriage.

The really good news for us is that we don't have to do the same as past generations. We can learn to manage our energies differently in our relationships, and we can teach our kids these skills as well. In families, we can teach each other how we want to be handled when someone is angry with us. And we can also learn how family members want us to approach them with our own anger.

When people in relationships begin to recognize anger first as an opportunity to learn about themselves and each other, and second as a chance to grow in the relationship, they can create the attitude of resolution and learn to stay connected throughout the anger/resolution process. And once we accomplish that, we will no longer feel so threatened by our anger or the anger of others.

What the message is really about. Anger happens. It's a fact of life, and the more we understand and work with it for productive outcomes, the better off we will be. Here are a few precepts to come back to again and again as you continue to make headway in using anger to create safety and connection in your relationships.

1. Accept that anger happens many times throughout the day to all of us.
2. Expect to feel anger often and know that is normal, not "bad."
3. Become acutely aware when you use rage or silence instead of addressing your anger with target-specific language.
4. Learn to look underneath your anger for the pain it is covering and be willing to share that awareness with your partner.
5. Use your anger as an opportunity to learn about yourself. When we are angry, we usually are projecting our own unresolved issues onto others.
6. Learn to state specifically and positively what you are wanting and needing instead of what you are getting.
7. Be prepared and willing to work with others when they are angry with you. This will require a previously agreed-upon plan from both parties about how to specifically choreograph this new process.

8. Learn to stay connected during the resolution process. This requires that both parties set a plan of action together for when either is feeling a disconnection in the relationship .
9. Be thankful for the gift of anger and respect its power in relationships, remembering that anger offers one of our best opportunities to grow past our old woundedness.

In order to do the above steps, we have to be able to *hold the tension of our discomfort instead of reacting to it*. Sitting with our discomfort instead of reacting to defend ourselves against it is an advanced, learned adult behavior. All of us have significant difficulty mastering this skill. Once we become aware of how much it can improve our relationships, however, and begin to *build the belief system* that it will work for us, we then claim the energy to pursue this path and stretch into new growth.

We all come wired with the right equipment to know and recognize our anger, and we have the ability and opportunities to handle our anger in ways differently than we were taught or shown as children. Our anger is an important energy of our personal power. Learning to use anger as it was initially designed for us—as a vital source of practical information and powerful, positive energy—can help us *move out of the "Victim Box."* Finding better ways to manage anger will help us learn that we do have choices, and that we are the masters of our fate. We are bigger than our anger and any other feeling we might have. We always have the choice as to how we will handle our feelings—all of them, especially anger.

Only victims live at the mercy of their feelings and other people's feelings. As adults, none of us has to remain a victim. We can *choose* healthier ways of being in relationships, by learning to connect with *all* our feelings and manage our anger with intentional, conscious behaviors instead of knee-jerk reactivity. In all of this work, our goal is to move up into that adult place that allows us to see our options and make the best choices for a responsible, connected relationship.

Chapter 4

Emotional Safety in Committed Love Relationships

"How do we get back to the good stuff?"

When we human beings feel emotionally safe with each other, we are relaxed, interactive, communicating without hesitation, intimately involved in a positive way, with very few of our defenses operating.

On the other hand, when we feel less than emotionally safe with each other, we are guarded, defensive, and aware of danger, feeling threatened and ready to move into our own full defense at any moment.

It's easy to take emotional safety for granted in relationships. We expect it to be there; it's what we want and need. We aren't usually aware of it in a conscious, intellectual way, but when a relationship is emotionally safe, we feel it, just as we feel the absence of that safety. In committed love relationships, establishing and maintaining the emotional safety both partners need and expect becomes more difficult, because as each partner finds ways to survive within the relationship, their very means of doing so can scare their partner nearly to death.

This dynamic of defenses between partners is one of the criteria described by Harville Hendrix as an "IMAGO match" (see the Resource List at the back of the book). As Hendrix explains it, the IMAGO theory is "guided by the belief that the primary sources of conflict in committed love relationships are the unseen, unresolved childhood wounds brought to the partnership by each individual. It is proposed that committed love has a hidden, unconscious purpose to heal these wounds. Conflict is viewed as not only inevitable but necessary to begin the journey into the healing process, for imbedded in a couple's frustrations lies the information necessary for healing and growth."

Part of the information needed is exposed as each partner survives within the relationship. The defenses one partner uses will arouse the other partner's worst fears, and that dynamic works in both directions. As we lose the element of emotional safety in the love relationship, which happens at some point as partners try to differentiate or be separate people, we forfeit all the "good stuff"—the pleasurable experiences that can happen within the perimeters of an emotionally safe, connected relationship. The "good stuff" encompasses the passion, fun, trust, intimacy, and attention we all long for in a love partner.

Romantic Love is not reality. Yet the emotional safety couples feel in Romantic Love before they marry is not a normal everyday state, but the result of chemicals produced naturally by heightened activity of certain areas of the brain. These chemicals, called *endorphins*, impart a wonderful sense of euphoria that allows both partners to believe they could never hurt each other. In fact, lovers often make that exact promise: "No one will ever be hurt in this relationship." Our starry-eyed lovers are making promises they can't keep, because the idealistic condition of Romantic Love is an artificial, chemically induced state produced in the brain, and at a certain point this euphoric state inevitably wears off. "The magic's gone," disillusioned lovers often say. And when that happens, both lovers begin to become aware that their partner can do and say hurtful things after all.

But while it lasts the euphoria these natural endorphins produce causes the lovers to run a private, personal, entirely positive "movie" inside their heads, each "movie" projecting an image of perfection upon the partner. This projected image causes them to experience a state of total mutual trust. They believe they are completely emotionally safe with each other forever.

As long as we enjoy this high degree of emotional safety, we can experience an unusually high level of passion and fun with our partner. We feel no fears, so we need no defenses. *All our energy can be spent on all the "good stuff" of the relationship:* affection, caring, nurturing, passion, sex, fun, playfulness, total freedom, abandonment of all fear or distrust of our partner. Nature produces this wonderful state long enough to persuade us to:

1) make a lifetime commitment to one love partner
2) recognize what we're missing when it wears off
3) strive ever after to get it back.

The only difference is that the next time we experience this wonderful state with our partner, rather than having it come upon us naturally and unbidden, with no effort on our part, we will have *worked* to get it. Right— once Romantic Love has faded, it takes *conscious, intentional work* to produce the next sustained experience of emotional safety with our partner.

Romantic Love ends, as it's supposed to do. Now, because we aren't familiar with this strange sequence of events that begins as Romantic Love, when the endorphins stop flowing and the internal "movie" is no longer projecting perfection onto our partner, we become aware that all that "good stuff" we had with our partner before is missing. All that delightful affection, attention, passion, and carefree sex is gone, but we don't relate this to our lack of emotional safety in the relationship.

All we know is that things have changed, and the only way we know to address this unsettling change is to hammer away at our partner in some fashion, trying to get the good feelings back. We may attack and accuse our partner of not caring any more, failing to see how threatening we have become in our own behavior and demeanor. If that's what's happening, the last thing our partner can think about is getting back to the "good stuff." All he or she can think about is how to *escape* the complaints and criticism—the very opposite of what the complaining partner is hoping for.

The Power Struggle begins. *This sequence of events is natural and should be expected at some point in a committed love relationship.* Technically, all that has happened is that the couple has moved from the Romantic Love stage to the stage of the Power Struggle. Both stages are supposed to happen, and they are supposed to come to an end. But if the couple doesn't understand and expect this change, when the Power Struggle hits they become terribly disillusioned and usually conclude that they married the wrong person.

In the Power Struggle, both partners become aware of each other's hurtful behavior. As one partner begins to defend himself or herself against being hurt, those very defenses alert the other partner that the emotional safety is gone from the relationship. Consequently, that partner, too, begins to put up defenses. It becomes a vicious cycle. The dance has begun. Each time a defensive behavior happens, the other partner reacts with more defenses. This can go on indefinitely. *Romantic Love was all about "the other," whereas the Power Struggle becomes all about "me."*

If I don't like the way my partner is treating or relating to me, my natural tendency is to ask him to change his behavior. But before I do that, I may want to consider the possibility that he's reacting out of feelings of emotional *unsafety*. Expecting someone else to change merely because I demand it is unrealistic. In fact, I can't change another person, I can only change myself. A more responsible approach is to try *asking myself* these questions:

- How might I have interrupted the emotional safety in our relationship, so that my partner feels a need for protection from me?

- If my partner no longer seems interested in affection, attention, and sex, what might I have said or done to arouse his or her defensive reaction?

- Is something I am saying or doing causing my partner to feel *unsafe* in our relationship, so that he or she is staying too busy or distanced or sick, too depressed, or otherwise unavailable to be with me?

Once Romantic Love fades, both partners tend to become careless about violating each other's emotional safety, taking that safety for granted. They don't see that emotional safety is what allows them to experience the "good stuff." Instead, they turn their thinking around and credit the affection, attention, sex, and passion for the good feelings of safety. Those things certainly feel good, but the *emotional safety is what allows them to happen* in any long-term, committed, love relationship.

Partners often don't even know what emotional safety is, or that it is always operating at some level within their relationship. Until it gets violated, they aren't aware that they need to have it in order to experience the good things in their relationship, and then they feel angry and threatened, because they realize something is missing. "You don't love me any more," is the usual complaint, provoking the target of that accusation to marshal all of his or her emotional defenses.

A more honest expression would be, "I don't feel emotionally safe with you any more, and I'm scared of losing your love." We have to be taught, however, to communicate with a partner in such a healthy way.

Some of the ways the Power Struggle plays out. Here's one typical "dance" we can observe in traditional relationships in our society. Partners violate each other emotionally time and again, usually without even knowing they're doing it. Yet, when one partner tries to tell the other that she feels scared or threatened, instead of speaking up that clearly, she might say, "You don't love me any more," or "I just don't feel the same excitement as when we were dating." Then that partner reacts: "That's not true! You don't feel that way, because I've given you no reason to feel that way, so get over it!"

So, the scared or threatened partner tries to get over it—deny the reality of her feelings—but she can't do it. She feels more afraid and finds it more and more difficult to give her partner all the good things they once shared in their relationship. As one partner draws away from the other or becomes more restricted about the good stuff (affection, connection, passion, and fun), the other grows more insistent, accusing the withholding partner of being cold and maybe even frigid. And as one becomes more insistent, the other feels more threatened and withholds even more. The insistent partner, feeling even more left out and neglected, demands more attention, while the withholding partner feels devalued, controlled, and overwhelmed. What a vicious cycle! To the persons caught up in it, it feels hopeless and depressing. As you can see, the emotional safety in this scenario is almost nonexistent, yet neither partner feels responsible for its absence. Both are so involved in self-protection, they can't see how it's their own defenses that are threatening the relationship.

This is a difficult dynamic for any of us to understand. If I don't mean to hurt you (especially if I'm only trying to defend my own hurt), how in the world can that be hurtful to you? Eventually partners have to accept the fact that they *do* hurt each other, usually unknowingly, just by *the nature of their own protective energies.*

A home-grown example. I can remember a time when I would ask my husband, just home from work, "Did you pick up the cleaning?"

That question, or the mere way I asked it, could easily set him off, and he would come back with a very defensive question: "Just what do you mean by that?"

All I wanted was a simple "Yes" or "No" response, so if necessary I could run out that evening or the next day to pick up the cleaning. I was speaking from my own agenda, asking what seemed to me a simple question with no other objective than getting an answer that would let me know how to proceed.

To my husband, though, my question felt like something entirely different, because he had a father who would ask him questions in such a way as to "trap" him, "catch" him in a lie or some form of manipulation of the facts. Therefore, almost any question I asked him would be received defensively, as if I were trying to trap or catch him, too. He seldom answered any question forthrightly but resorted to a defensive question of his own.

We danced this dance hundreds of times in our life together until we were able to gain some insight into what was really going on. My question felt accusing or blaming to him, like the questions his father used to ask, and I needed to be aware of that and be responsible for choosing my actions and framing my questions in a way he could accept. The only way we managed to solve this puzzle was by talking about it, me expressing my bewilderment about not understanding how I was hurting him and him sharing information with me about his own family history . Without that knowledge of why my questions provoked such a defensive stance, we could never have figured it out. Once he realized how powerful his dad's quizzing of him was in our present-day marriage, he could make a conscious choice about how to handle my questions and teach me to question him in ways that did not alert his Old Brain (Unconscious Mind) to defend against Dad.

What seems perfectly innocent, sensible, or ordinary to one partner can often be very hurtful to the other partner, and sometimes for the most unimaginable reasons. Here's another example of how our "innocent" behavior hurts our partner, because of something in their history. My husband always liked to serve my plate at the table. To him this was a thoughtful, loving gesture, yet inwardly it sent me up the wall. I didn't stop him, but it irritated me. I was not consciously aware of how much it bothered me until many years down the matrimonial road. Finally, I spoke up and told him I didn't want him to serve my plate, to please serve his own and allow me to serve mine. My request baffled him, because he perceived his action as caring, doing something special for me.

It took me a long time to figure out which "nerve" that behavior was hitting from my history, which old family tape it was replaying. When I did figure it out and told my husband, he totally understood. Thereafter he honored my history and put his own opinion aside. Here's why it bothered me so much.

When I was a child, my dad would always serve my plate, then make me eat everything he put on it, even if it made me gag or actually throw up. I had to continue eating until every morsel was gone, and sometimes the portions were far too large for a child. So when my husband served my plate, it brought up those old feelings of being controlled and overwhelmed.

The point is, we come from different histories, bringing lots of invisible baggage with us. Partners must learn to honor and respect each other's history and be willing to alter their hurtful behavior accordingly. What bothers one partner may not even faze the other, because they have different histories. If it weren't for our histories and the unfinished hurts that lurk in their depths, some things might bother us a little, but never with the power they have to hurt us when one of our old historical raw nerves is hit by someone we love.

Incidentally, when it came time for my husband to ask me for special treatment, guess what he requested? Yes, to serve his plate for him! Which I did with a smile, knowing that I would also be serving my own.

Voice our distress, or stuff it? A person who expects to act however he pleases without ever hurting his partner lives in a fantasy world. Partners inevitably hurt or distress one another. And when they do, if the partner being hurt doesn't speak up, and the hurtful behavior continues, resentment builds, until ultimately there is an explosion, a divorce, or something far worse.

Whenever my partner speaks to me or treats me in a way that, although it makes sense to him, is hurtful or threatening to me, I have a *responsibility* to let him know so we can find a better way. By not speaking up, I am allowing the emotional safety in the relationship to be damaged or lost. The result will be distance and disconnection between the two of us, which is the last thing I want in our relationship.

We must be willing to speak up and find ways to work with our partners to help them understand what they are saying or doing that is causing discomfort in our relationship. Unless we do this, disruption of the emotional safety will result—then there goes the "good stuff."

Reclaiming emotional safety. *As we saw earlier, when Romantic Love fades and partners' emotional safety begins to evaporate, getting the good stuff back happens because the couple works for it.* It doesn't come by magic, or by wishing it would, because relationship skills have to be learned.

The answer to the title question of this chapter, "How do we get back to the good stuff?" is that we reestablish the connection in the relationship by recreating the emotional safety. One way of doing this is by means of a special exercise designed by Harville Hendrix, called "Intentional Dialogue." I teach this exercise without fail in my work with couples and families and often see emotional safety miraculously restored when these simple steps are followed *consistently.*

Without emotional safety, partners have no energy available to learn and grow, because they are too busy defending themselves. But once partners begin to feel safe again in a relationship, free of the need to stay on the defensive, they become willing to learn and do the essential relationship work. When emotional safety is restored, a spirit of cooperation and willingness emerges. I refer to this human condition as "becoming teachable and workable."

Intentional Dialogue is a learned communication skill that can serve as the first step in helping couples learn about each other as unique individuals. It provides the connection material necessary to build bridges between partners and allows them to operate from a "WE" perspective. Here is how is goes. The person speaking will be called the *Sender,* the person responding will be called the *Receiver.*

1. The *Sender* begins by saying something about herself to the Receiver, not to exceed two sentences.
2. The *Receiver* listens well enough that he mirrors the partner's words back verbatim, then asks, "Did I get that?"
   If the *Sender* says "Yes," they go on to the next step.

If the *Sender* says, "No," the *Receiver* asks the *Sender,* "Please send the message again" or "Tell me what I missed."

They stay with the message until the *Receiver* can repeat it verbatim.

3. After the *Receiver* has accurately mirrored back the *Sender's* words, the next step is to validate those words unconditionally.

   Receiver validates with either "I understand that" or "That makes sense."

   After the message has been validated unconditionally, if the *Receiver* does not understand even a part of what is being said, he can say, "Tell me more" until the *Receiver* begins to understand at least some of the message. Each time, the *Receiver* will mirror *Sender's* words verbatim and validate them unconditionally.

4. The next step is for the *Receiver* to offer genuine empathy by saying, "I imagine you are feeling_____" and supply a word that might describe your partner's feelings, then ask, "Does that fit?" That word may or may not fit.

   Sender will answer with a "Yes" when the word does fit, and *Receiver* will repeat the word and validate unconditionally with "I understand that" or "That makes sense."

   If the *Sender* says, "No, that doesn't really fit" or is hesitant to accept the word presented by the *Receiver, Receiver* then says, "Could you give me a better word?" and waits for *Sender* to supply the more accurate feeling word.

   Receiver repeats partner's word and validates it unconditionally. That's the end of the exercise.

Requiring the *Receiver* to repeat the *Sender's* words verbatim may sound artificial and strict. While you're learning this exercise, however, the verbatim rule serves the purpose of 1) slowing the *Sender* down so that the *Receiver* is not overloaded with verbiage, and 2) giving the *Receiver* the opportunity to listen for the exact language the partner uses to describe his or her world.

For most of us this is a new experience—being heard precisely the way we speak and in clearly stated increments. In ordinary dialogue, the listening partner has a natural tendency to reword the other's expressions, give an opinion, make a judgment, or offer advice on what we was heard. In this exercise none of that happens. Each partner works consciously to concentrate and do the job of the *Sender* or *Receiver.* And on the unconscious level, this exercise is very soothing to the Old Brain, keeping it calm—no fight-or-flight reaction is evoked. Thus both partners remain *emotionally safe* and can stay present with each other without becoming reactive.

The *Receiver's* job in this exercise is to constantly send the message of emotional safety to his partner, ensuring that he will listen and not react. It's his responsibility to repeat exactly what he hears without questioning, judging, or reacting in any way, then to validate those words unconditionally. The *Receiver* finishes by adding the element of empathy, trying to imagine how the partner might have felt or be feeling about those words she was speaking.

The *Sender* bears the responsibility of holding her energy at tolerable levels without attacking or aggressively provoking their partner with her words. She conveys a constant message that she is committed to the relationship and to the effort it takes *to speak about it in such a way that the connection will not be broken.* It is also the *Sender's* responsibility to help the *Receiver* hear and accurately mirror what she says.

What is validation? Validation does not mean the two partners agree, or even that one partner's statements make sense to the other. Unconditional validation means allowing space for the partner's reality in the relationship, each partner understanding that the other is a different and unique person, free to think and express himself or herself in ways that are different from the partner's ways. A partner is sending the message: I am using my energy to understand your world—instead of reacting to what you are saying—as I hope you will try to understand me.

What is empathy? Empathy creates the actual connection between partners, because in order to even express genuine empathy, we must be available to hear another's reality and be vulnerable enough to connect to their different world. Empathy means moving into the "as if" place described by Carl Rogers how it might feel for me to be in your place. We can never actually be in the shoes of another. Even if we have the same biological parents and were raised in the same home together, we all experience that same home differently. So, empathy is not about understanding exactly how someone else might feel, because that's never truly possible. Empathy is about listening well enough to another, without the interference of our own reality, and imagining how we might feel "as if" we were in that other's place.

Empathy is also a form of compassion, of reaching far enough into the world of another person that we can feel for and with them. Empathy is not a place of "poor you" or pity. With pity, we move ourselves *above* another and *look down* upon others with condescending sympathy. Even the simple art of listening and mirroring back what you hear someone say is a form of empathy. Empathy is making the effort to hear someone else's reality without interjecting our own or trying to manipulate theirs to make ourselves feel more comfortable.

Genuine empathy happens when a person allows himself *to open up* as he hears the reality of another and realizes his own vulnerability around the issues he hears from the other person. *We bond with another person in our vulnerable places, not our strengths.* When we are focused on our strengths, we *compete.* When we are in touch with our vulnerabilities, we *bond.* Bonding is the connection that happens when two or more people realize they both have a similar hurt place. We realize we are not isolated in our pain—that we are probably normal—and this relieves us of our shame about hurting and having needs around our pain.

That is one of the strongest attributes of Twelve-Step Groups, serving as an arena where we can relate to others' vulnerabilities and allow them to relate to ours. As Maya Angelou has said, "Telling our truth reminds us of how alike we are as humans." My guess is that we only *seem* different because we *hide* so much of the truth of who we really are.

Chapter 5

What Is Reality?

"Where did you ever come up with such an idea?"

In the area of relationships, when we speak of a person's reality, we're talking about something subjective, individual, unique, and impossible for another person to experience or duplicate. Our reality is what makes us who we are, how we view the world, how we experience life with other people, how we interact in our world and survive any threats to our perceptions of the world and how we believe it operates. No two people can have the same reality. Even children raised in the same home by the same biological parents have different realities, because they experienced life differently in that home with those parents. My reality will never be identical with yours, nor will yours be identical with mine.

Our reality is made up of our history, personal experience, what we have watched or heard about others experiencing, our knowledge, education, social conditioning, emotions, hopes, dreams, and literally anything that has ever touched our lives since we began to form as a human being before birth.

All of this information is fed onto a huge "reel"—our brain—that keeps a "movie" running for us twenty-four hours of every day, even while we sleep. That "movie" is our projection of the reality we know, and it colors whatever we view, experience, feel, and try to take in as being real. Any information or data about to enter our brain will first be washed through our existing reality and colored by it, so that we can take the new material in and integrate it with what we already believe to be the truth about our world.

Our reality determines how we perceive what is happening to us and what we are seeing, hearing, experiencing, enduring, enjoying. It's the deciding factor in what we *make of* what we see, hear, experience, endure, enjoy. Our reality sorts out everything touching our lives and gives us meanings to assign to our experiences. The way we sort depends upon the content on our "projector reels," what we already have in our own personal history bank, experience, knowledge, emotions, hopes, dreams, and even our imaginations.

Reality's other side. Although a large part of our reality is unknown to us in a conscious way, as we operate in life, others can often see that we may have some other agenda operating than the stated one. At times we even wonder ourselves why we have acted in a certain way or made a particular decision. Frequently others describe us using words that we don't believe fit us at all.

I remember a time in high school when someone writing for our school newspaper described me as "fastidious." I didn't know what it meant, so I looked it up and discovered it meant "picky, hard to please, perfectionistic." I was astounded, because in my family of obsessive-compulsive perfectionists, I was considered a slob! Viewing the world from my reality, I believed I was the easiest person in the world to please, as compared to everyone else in my family. Yet to the outside world, or at least from the viewpoint of that particular writer's reality, I was perceived as just the opposite.

I didn't want to believe it then, but the time did come when I had to look at my own obsessive-compulsive perfectionism. That writer knew what she was talking about in describing me and could see in me what I wasn't able to see.

Why honest feedback is crucial. This variance in personal reality is one reason why it is so important for couples to give each other honest feedback. Each of us needs one or more caring persons in our life who are willing to tell us how they experience us and how our behavior affects them, so that we can alter aspects of it to be less hurtful, thoughtless, or insensitive.

We do not experience ourselves as others do. *In fact, it is impossible for me to experience myself as others do. Our life experience comes from behind our own eyes, and the best way we have of learning more about ourselves is to listen openly to others when they tell us how they experience us and try to imagine how that must feel to them.*

And once we have heard their feedback, we can ask for and accept their suggestions as to how we can alter our hurtful behavior. The choice of altering it or not is always up to us.

How we hurt each other unintentionally. We see life *behind our own eyes*—from our own reality—and most of us never intend to be hurtful, thoughtless, or insensitive. At times, nevertheless, we are all of those things, regardless of our intent. As life experiences enter our space of perception, they pass through the filter of our reality before we assign a meaning to them or even understand from within our own reality what we have just encountered.

What may be funny to one person can be sad to another, or what might be insensitive to one person could be thoughtful to another. The intent of the person sending a message and the meaning assigned to it by the receiver are often totally different. The sender does not usually intend to be hurtful, acting and speaking in ways that make good sense to them. But the receiver assigns his or her own personal meaning to the sender's words or behaviors and decides for himself whether or not it felt hurtful.

Because we were all wounded differently by a variety of people, our definitions of what is wounding will vary greatly. Here's an example. Pat was constantly feeling hurt because her husband Paul seemed to not listen to her. He would walk away when she was talking, read the paper and grunt "Uh-huh" sporadically, or watch TV. He wasn't meaning to offend her, and he could actually repeat back to her some of what she had just said. To Pat, however, his behavior and body language said, "What you're saying is so unimportant that I don't need to pay attention!"

Yet Paul saw it another way. He prided himself on being able to multi-task—to listen and attend to other things at the same time. And he had another, hidden agenda. Paul hated unpleasantness, and he hoped if he didn't appear attentive, then Pat wouldn't bring up any unpleasant issues. If he seemed preoccupied and a little busy, perhaps she'd conclude it wasn't a good time for serious topics. He justified his behavior by the fact that they had been able to avoid a lot of unpleasantness in their marriage. So both Pat and Paul were continually uncomfortable—she feeling unheard, Paul always afraid something touchy would come up.

How I feel is up to me. When you tell someone that what they said hurt your feelings, and the person replies, "Well, it shouldn't have, because I didn't mean it as hurtful," that person is assigning feelings to *you* out of *their* reality. It doesn't change how you feel. These dynamics are part of what complicates relationships.

Parents do this all the time. They assign to their children whatever feelings they want them to have, and actually expect their assignment to change their kids' feelings!

Mom says, "You shouldn't be mad at your father, you know he had to work late and couldn't make your game." Is the child still mad, and maybe hurt too? Sure. Only now he will be doubly mad, because Mom tried to manipulate his feelings by shaming him for having them.

Trying to force another person to see life through our eyes doesn't work. Not only does that person feel controlled and his feelings invalidated, he or she also feels wrong and ashamed for even having those feelings. If someone's attitude about a situation ever changes, it's because he decided to change it, not because you made him change it.

We do not have the power to change anyone's feelings unless they decide to let that happen.

What is normal? Another factor that forms our reality is whatever we grew up with in our families of origin. Whatever crazy things might have been happening in our families at home, we accepted them as *normal* in order to survive and grow up. In my own family of origin, our "normal" day included an angry, abusive, alcoholic father who scared all of us nearly to death with his explosive temper and physical aggression.

Our mother never stopped him or tried to interfere with his tirades, probably because she was afraid, too, and her own reality told her that the man of the house had a sacred position ordained by God. As a result, my sister and I learned to view this horror story as somewhat normal! We didn't try to interfere with his inappropriate behavior nor with our mom's lack of protection. We *normalized* it in order to survive. But in order to assimilate so much inappropriateness into our realities, we had to skew our realities to accommodate his intolerable behavior.

When you add to this the principle that rules every home with an active alcoholic or addict—"Don't *ever* talk outside these four walls about what happens here!"—we didn't talk about what was going on to anybody else, including other family members who might could have helped us figure out whether our home life was normal or not.

Children learn what they live. So it should come as no surprise that my sister and I grew up with an infinite capacity for tolerating inappropriate behavior in others, which has hurt us in all our relationships. We spent a large part of our lives either acting as inappropriately as our dad, plowing over others' personal boundaries, or else emulating our mom in not setting limits when others chose to treat us with their own versions of inappropriateness.

Your expectations, my expectations. As all of us grow from children to adults, we will form a reality of our own and also accommodate the history within our parents' realities, which most of us usually don't even consciously know. As we do this, forming our own reality, we slowly accept a view of the world warped by what our environment has exposed us to. Maybe I'm making this process sound complicated or scary, but it actually is the way that we emerge in life with a formed reality of our own.

I remember when our kids were growing up, I would say to my husband, "Let's take a vacation with the kids and go somewhere really adventuresome." He'd say, "No, I don't think that would be a good idea, because we don't need to be spending that kind of money on a holiday!" He was serious, and I couldn't figure out why we needed to save 90 cents out of every dollar. He acted like we were about to go under financially any minute when it came to what he considered "frivolous" spending.

We danced this shuffle for years without realizing what it was really about. Then, as I listened to my husband's parents talk about their lives, they both mentioned the Great Depression often and how hard they'd struggled to survive. His mom was especially frightened about being poor again, and his father's mother liked to hold actual money in her hand to reassure herself that they had some. So over the years it finally dawned on me that my husband had listened to the recital of his family's very real economic struggles to the point that he had *internalized* their experience as his own.

One day I said to him, "You know, your parents lived through the Great Depression, but we didn't. That was them, this is us. We've always had enough money, and we can actually afford to take a nice holiday with the kids. Let's go!"

After he thought about this message he had lived with all his life, he decided the Depression was not his experience after all and that we could afford a nice trip with the kids.

Do you see how our parents' realities and experiences influence our own? In order to become mature human beings we have to become conscious of what belongs to *us* as *our* experience, integrate that into our reality, and leave what belongs to our parents back with them.

Whose truth? Once we understand the psychological concepts that form a person's reality, we can more easily recognize that no one on this planet holds The Truth, The Whole Truth, and Nothing But The Truth. Everyone's truth is The Truth to him or her, but not to anyone else.

When I came to understand this, I was finally able to disagree with or confront another person's "truth" that had a negative influence on my life. I hope that it will help you too, too, that one person's "truth" is merely that person's reality and nothing more, regardless of how *entitled* the person might feel to be the possessor of "The Truth" for our universe.

As we learn this and put it into practice in our lives, we will become more able to speak our own "truth" with entitlement and confidence, recognizing all the while that we occupy only a tiny, separate space on this planet with that "truth." Once we learn to relax a little around each other's opinions, beliefs, and points of views, we can then listen more openly to another with the knowledge that what we are hearing is merely that person's reality, which is no more important than ours, yet is just as important to him or to her as mine is to me.

I often tell clients, "Picture my truth as a *fly on the back of an elephant's butt*. My truth is no greater or smaller than yours, even though I may speak my truth with authority and passion. Just keep picturing that fly. Hear me out, then give me your truth—which is *also* a fly on the back of an elephant's butt."

And of course the same image applies when we're expressing our version of truth to a partner and listening to the partner's version.

You see, we believe our realities to be true, and they are—but only in relevance to us and to our world, which *lies only behind our own eyes.*

When we accept the world only as we experience it from within our own reality, when we see only One Truth and it is ours, we eliminate the rest of the world. Nobody has a monopoly on truth, because it's different for every one of us. Often when we experience people as being very different from us, our only relief is to say they are "crazy" to be the way they are. Yet in fact they are merely *different* from us.

This is the Hatfields-and-McCoys experience. When people see life from a perspective so different from ours, to us, "They're crazy. Don't talk to them, don't listen, or try to understand their world, just shoot 'em!" And mayhem is the result.

Watching how all of us operate with our different realities can be extremely interesting. No matter what a person does, says, or expresses, it makes sense to that person at that moment, else they wouldn't be doing it. Acting ridiculous or crazy *on purpose* makes us too vulnerable to risk it, unless we're intentionally entertaining.

The challenge is to listen attentively as others give us the context around their reality, which lies within their words and their behaviors. When we practice opening up and allowing ourselves to relax about how different we all are, it becomes a fascinating experiment. If we try to really hear another person's reality without needing to change it or alter it, we may learn to tolerate that person. *We may even become able to believe that their reality is just as valid as ours.*

So can we all do whatever we please? Of course not. Just because we all have different realities doesn't mean we can do away with laws and moral codes. Learning to accept one another's different realities does not mean we must excuse or tolerate inappropriate behaviors.

The realities of some people may be so skewed that, to them, breaking the laws or violating the moral codes we need on this planet can seem perfectly reasonable and justified. In those cases, we generally rely on the courts to step in and decide a "right" and "wrong." In a court of law, decisions are based on the law's truth as to "right" or "wrong," "good' or "bad," "innocent" or "guilty." That's as it should be. In relationships, however, different standards prevail, because each partner's reality—each partner's "truth"—is relevant to that individual's history and life experience.

We all have different realities, and we are all responsible for how we live them out. Our different realities don't excuse us from any behavior that is less than appropriate or does harm to other people. As we recognize how our realities vary, however, and how many different perspectives we all bring to life, we may come to see what a tremendous job we have in living together in this world. Of course it's a challenge, but the benefits are worth the work it takes to get them.

Health of the relationship is the goal. Sometimes couples come to therapy for me to declare one partner "guilty" or "crazy" or "wrong" or "bad." But that's not my job. In a relationship between two people trying to build a life together, the truth of both partners must be heard and validated, because it takes two people to make a relationship and two people to tear it up. In couples' therapy, we work for the health of the relationship, whatever will enable it to endure and grow strong. I believe that, regardless to whom you're married, something within your own energies will allow you to tolerate that relationship, no matter how unhappy you might be. So the place to begin relationship work is with that energy within each partner that has allowed the relationship to get to where it is, instead of simply blaming your partner for all the problems.

What about boundaries? Related to our differing realities is the need for boundaries. Emotionally healthy people understand that, because we are so different in the way we perceive this world that learning to set and hold healthy, personal boundaries is vital—boundaries that are emotional, physical, sexual, intellectual, and spiritual.

People who see no need for healthy personal boundaries persist in believing that everyone sees life through the same scope—*theirs*—and expect us all to conform to their limited view of the world. Since these people also believe that they hold the one "true" reality on this planet, in their opinion, whatever makes sense to them should also make sense to those whose boundaries they cross.

If such a person feels a need to talk disrespectfully to you because you don't seem to understand him or her—you're probably stating some disagreement with that person's views—the offender sanctions the disrespectful behavior as "necessary" and does whatever he or she considers "necessary" to open your eyes to "The Truth" (theirs, of course). Unable or unwilling to perceive their *own* need for personal boundaries, they cannot imagine that you or anyone else would have or need personal boundaries.

If you are a person who sometimes makes blanket statements as if you possess the sole truth, or as if speaking with the voice of God, you may want to practice getting comfortable with this concept of differing realities by working at changing your language a bit. Try modifying your statements by prefacing them with such openings as "It's my opinion that . . . " or "It's my belief that . . . " or "From my reality, it seems to me . . . " or "It's my experience that . . . " And that is all it is—your opinion, belief, reality, or experience, no more or less valid than everyone else's.

Bringing it all home. One day my grown daughter and I were having a disagreement. Her voice was raised, and I asked, "Why do you need to be in my face yelling?" She shot back, "I'm not yelling!" I said, "Yes, you are." She yelled again, "No, I'm not!" I said, "YES, YOU ARE!" She barked back, **"NO, I'M NOT!"**

After three rounds of this, I remembered to say, "I'm *experiencing you* as yelling, and you can't have my experience!" She instantly calmed down and said, "Oh, yeah! That is true." Because she's learning this concept of different realities and separate truths, I finally got her attention when I pointed out I was reporting *my experience of her.* Did you notice it took me until the fourth try to find the appropriate words?

This is an opportunity for couples and other family members to speak individually, from their own reality, about how they experience each other in positive and negative ways. If someone wants to challenge your experience, they can do so, but you can also remind the person that none of us experiences ourselves as others experience us.

We all experience ourselves from behind our own eyes. It's impossible to have another person's experience of me!

Chapter 6

What Our Past Can Teach

"Get Mom and Dad out of the china cabinet!"

Does that chapter title grab you? I hope so, because the subject has huge implications for us all. Every experience we've ever had is a thread in the big tapestry that makes us who we are today. We can remember the good experiences with pleasure, fortunately, and build on them as we move on. And we can try—*try*—to sweep unpleasant experiences under the rug, but they will always come back to haunt us until we deal with them. And the primary way they affect us is in our relationships, especially the ones where we want to feel connected and loved.

Alice Miller, Ph.D., has been the great champion of this subject. She has written book after book on the dangers of idolizing our parents and refusing to look honestly at our early childhood experiences, especially the unpleasant ones.

My expression for this is "keeping Mom and Dad in the china cabinet" as a way of describing what she means. Here's how Alice Miller puts it:

The more we idolize the past and refuse to acknowledge our childhood sufferings, the more we pass them on unconsciously to the next generation.

The more we idolize the past, the less likely we are to look back and discover our own unmet emotional needs. And if we don't even recognize that we *have* unmet emotional needs, we can't understand how those unfinished parts of our emotional development impact our present-day relationships, especially with our partners and our children.

Denying our emotional damage. By denying that we were ever emotionally damaged, we continue to perpetuate the damage that was done to us and that we do to others. If we aren't in touch with the woundedness that endures in us from childhood hurts, we have no awareness of how wounding we are to others, especially those we love. This is why I stress with each couple: "The best hope for you and your partner is to get Mom and Dad out of the china cabinet and discover your childhood wounding, so that the damage to your relationship can stop."

Let me clarify what I mean by "woundedness" and another related expression, "emotional dependency needs." Emotional dependency needs refer to every human being's drive to feel unconditionally loved, emotionally and physically safe, significant, capable, accepted and enjoyed for who we are—our longing to feel heard and unconditionally validated. We all need to believe we can make some difference on this earth, that we can effect change, and that we belong.

When pain happens around any of these needs as we seek to get them met, woundedness occurs. You might be thinking, "Those needs aren't even realistic, they can never be completely and unconditionally met." I agree with you, they can't be perfectly met, because we don't have any perfect people yet to meet them. But the fact remains that we still experience *emotional wounding* every time they don't get met. We carry in our bodies this unresolved pain from our wounding, and regardless of our intentions and desires, it always seeps out into our relationships.

By *unresolved pain*, I mean any feelings that were never dealt with, never recognized, never talked about or validated. Unresolved pain is attached to any subject that we knew never to bring up, mention, notice, see, hear, or speak about, because if we did, the big people would get upset, angry, disappointed, silent, distant, anxious, or have some other unpleasant feeling.

All children have a magical expectation that their needs will be met. No wonder, because during the nine months (or however long) we lived as fetuses inside our mother's body, all our needs were met without our even having to ask.

And then as babies in our cribs we began to realize that when we cried loud enough and long enough, the big people came and met our physical needs. At least this is how it worked for those of us who survived to adulthood. As we grew up, our parents anticipated some of our needs—mostly physical ones—and helped us get those met. So, by the time we reached adulthood, we had internalized this expectation that *our needs would be met for us by other people or other things.*

But our parents failed to teach us one crucial lesson—*as adults, we ourselves are responsible for getting most of our own needs met.* As adults, we meet most of our physical needs without much conscious thought. Yet when it comes to our emotional needs, we persist in believing that those are the responsibility of someone else. Actually, we're responsible for meeting about 80% of them; the other 20% are usually met by other people, our partners, our children, extended family, friends, work, and other relationships. Nevertheless, we continue to expect other people to "make us happy."

Thus, emotionally, we're still babies crying in our cribs, waiting for someone—usually our partners or kids—to come and meet those needs. Some people go so far, in fact, as to believe that making oneself happy is simply not possible. Because they believe their happiness is someone else's job, if someone else asks them to assume personal responsibility for being happy, they get resentful, believing that their partner or their family has betrayed them. The old saying is true, though: happiness is an inside job. We find happiness only when *we* decide to be happy.

Ways of dealing with our unspoken pain. We all like to think of ourselves as independent and self-sufficient, but the truth is that we have many unmet emotional needs, which leave us with an inner woundedness, an emotional emptiness. And in that woundedness we do all sorts of things to compensate for the pain. Once we commit ourselves to reach for greater maturity and emotional growth, we will address that lingering pain, seek to understand from whence it came, and grieve those losses, in order to move on with our lives in healthy ways.

If we continue blundering on, managing to ignore our pain and emotional woundedness, unwilling even to look at the possibility that we have unmet emotional needs, then we try to ease them with other anesthetics, mainly by getting lost in our addictions: work, money, exercise, gambling, food, religion, affairs, alcohol, other drugs. In other words, *we try everything other than recognizing and addressing the cause of that pain.*

When we consider the alternative—unhappiness and dissatisfaction with life—there's no doubt that digging into the past and getting those wounds healed is far and away the healthiest, most promising course. Yes, it's hard work. Yes, it's frequently painful, for short periods of time. But which would you choose, living with the chronic pain of appendicitis until it kills you, or letting the surgeon cut the diseased appendix out once and for all? Scars heal. Untreated emotional wounds do not.

Having our emotional dependency needs met is an innate drive in all human beings, and most of us suffer deep emotional pain when they are not met.

Denying our wounds. Why do we deny that we have such damage and wounds? Partly because to look at these wounds, we have to go to their original source—our families of origin—since those are our first emotional relationships. We feel a strong need to protect our parents, no matter what kind of parents they may have been. Because parents represent the means of survival to young children, children tend to view their parents as having godlike powers. By extension, in the mind of a child, any doubts about a parent's perfection is like doubting God's perfection. That's scary stuff, for if we start doubting God, maybe He won't help us survive.

Even grown children who are still dependent on their parents in some way— accepting money from them, for example—are quick to defend those flawed people, because their survival still depends on those parents. Flawed? Of course. All of us are flawed.

When an adult refuses to consider that his or her parents might have human flaws, one can't help wondering why those lives have to be so desperately protected from scrutiny or examination. When someone's family history is so fragile that they cannot tolerate examination or questioning about it, I want to ask them, "What really happened to Aunt Suzie? Or what is it about Uncle Ted that scares you to death?"

The power of family secrets. Our families think that if we never talk about those family secrets, they will fade away and not affect us. But that belief is only a myth passed down from generations to enable us to avoid facing up to unpleasantness. Those who insist on maintaining the family secrets don't recognize that a lot of the damage in the present-day family is old stuff that was never dealt with, and that all the skeletons we have obediently tiptoed around are not resting.

Family secrets rest in peace? No way. Life will present them to us again and again until someone picks up the ball and says, "No more! Enough!" and has the courage to talk, question, examine, and unravel the truth. John Bradshaw says it well in his book *Family Secrets*: "What one generation refuses to deal with will be passed down to the next generation."

Most adults do not understand the significance of examining their own family history and the people who have played parts in it. Just as when we go to a medical doctor, we are questioned about our medical history, in relationships we have an equally strong need to review our emotional history, because that's the history we recreate and repeat in our present-day lives. Consciously or unconsciously, we are driven to recreate what we know, because when we were children we accepted what we experienced as "normal," and what was hurtful is still unfinished.

Just imagine what it would be like to go to a medical doctor and have that doctor not want to hear any of our medical history, to refuse to hear whether anyone in our family had had heart trouble, cancer, diabetes, etc. And every time we opened our mouth to supply some piece of what we thought would be vital medical history about our family, this doctor would yell, "STOP! I don't want to hear any of that! I don't have to know those things in order to help you!" Wouldn't you be appalled and wonder what in the world was wrong with such a doctor? We most certainly wouldn't want such a person treating us.

That all-powerful emotional history. Knowing our own emotional history is just as important as knowing our medical history. Why? Because our emotional history can tell us a great deal about who we are today and why we operate as we do in our present relationships. *Emotional history is the main substance of which relationships are made.* When emotional needs are met, relationships work better. When emotional needs remain unmet, relationships stay stuck and painful and often end.

We cannot change what we are not even aware of, so one of the most important things to examine about myself is my history in relationships, starting with my very first serious relationships—those that happened in my family of origin. First and foremost is my relationship with my parents, and after that relationships to others in the family—siblings, aunts and uncles, grandparents, whoever had an influence on my early life.

Unmet emotional needs. Unwillingness to examine our past experiences, especially those from childhood when we had so few ways to defend ourselves against emotional pain, perpetuates one particularly toxic feeling—*self-hate*. In his book *Keeping the Love You Find*, Harville Hendrix contends that the beginnings of self-hate arise when children's emotional needs are unmet. Such children eventually begin to hate having *any* needs and will attribute their own neediness to some character flaw within themselves, which ultimately leads them to hate themselves. That self-hate continues to show up in our lives as we defeat and sabotage ourselves. The unmet needs attached to the self-hate must be brought into the light so that we can get honest and emotionally safe to those we love today.

Children clearly notice what adults are attending to in their own lives and the lives of their kids, and they are seeing adults who focus primarily on physical needs. So when a child's other needs aren't attended to—the emotional dependency needs to be hugged, nurtured, kept close, kept safe, defended—the child concludes that having those needs must somehow be wrong. By extension, the child comes to believe there is something wrong with *him*, else he wouldn't be having these needs. Such a child will hate that naturally needy part of himself and become ashamed of who he is. Never mind that he's a perfectly normal child with perfectly normal needs. He sees himself from that skewed reality, that world where emotional needs aren't met.

Denying our emotional needs. In working with clients, trying to help them get in touch with those basic unmet emotional dependency needs, I often find them very defensive about this whole subject. When I ask them to recount some wounding incident from childhood having to do with unmet emotional needs, they may respond in an extremely defensive way. Even the suggestion of looking back indicates blame:

"Why do you always have to blame everything on my childhood?" or

"I have no unpleasant memories from childhood!" or

"There's nothing unpleasant there to talk about!"

Or I might hear, "How many times are we going over this? You've heard about my childhood, and it was basically good. We're just wasting time!"

They might even try to dismiss me as their parents did them: "Okay, so it happened. But it wasn't a big deal. I think you're making too much of it." This person is reacting with exactly the same style of denial and defense her parents or caregivers used on her as a child, when her emotional needs surfaced. And she's probably even using the same language and holding the same attitude and position her parents used on her.

An example: Sara decided to finally tell her mom about her brother smoking pot and how worried she was about him. Mom's instant response was, "That just isn't true! Your brother's grades are good, and he just made the yearbook team. There can't be anything bad going on with him! Besides, he keeps telling me he's happy with his life, so clearly nothing bad can be going on."

Regardless of the parent's defensive style, the child's feelings are dismissed. It's interesting to hear the grown-up child talk from this same perspective, just as their parent talked to them: "Saundra, my parents did the best they could, and even if they did hurt me, they didn't mean to!" I don't doubt the statement. Parents don't normally mean to hurt their children, but the reality is that they do. All we parents do.

The more energy there is around the denial, the less likely it is that that child's parents recognized and helped that child get his or her emotional needs met. It may take a long while in therapy before such a client becomes willing to consider that his or her parents were imperfect human beings and acknowledge it by exploring their own history. Meanwhile, those wounded people continue wounding others without even realizing it.

Getting emotional needs met. On the other hand, if the person answers with a more realistic, less defensive, less energetic response, I take this as an indication that the person's parents did help him get some of his emotional needs met, and he is probably less wounding to those he loves in his own present-day relationships.

Getting emotional needs met is about getting your feelings validated, *exactly the way you experienced them.* This may be all that is required for the person to feel attended to and affirmed within his or her own reality. That is the full job and responsibility of the parents—validation of the child's reality and feelings—even though they might not agree with the child's perception of how it was. If they could just do that for the child, that *validation in and of itself is very healing for emotional pain*. It's very healing for all of us.

The lessons we learned as children when we took our troubles to our parents were sometimes hurtful. Without knowing a better way, parents may have either criticized, shamed, or dismissed those needs. So, the naturally needy child learned to hide his needs from others first, and then from himself. Subsequently he came to hate those needs, then hate himself for having such needs.

In the life of the adult child who's still having difficulty with relationships, such a person is often willing to deny his own truth in order to "save" or "respect" or "be loyal to" those poor parents who, like all of us, messed up. *These defenses keep us cut off from our own truth.* They teach us to hide from our own truth, just as our parents did. We learn to preserve the nice picture of perfection that our parents needed as a cover for their own imperfections, and in perpetuating the myth, we do the same damage to our kids and our partners as was done to us.

Are Mom and Dad still in the china cabinet? One of the indicators of whether a person still has her parents locked into that false picture of perfection is that she continually wounds others in her own relationships. She does this because she lacks empathy for them, unaware that her behavior is hurtful. When we choose not to examine our own experiences of life, starting with our childhoods, we deny a large part of our existence and reality. And the negative parts we deny in ourselves are the very things we criticize today in those with whom we want to be in relationship now . Instead of owning these negative parts of our selves, we attribute them to other people, especially those we love. The very thing that most annoys us in another person will be a characteristic we need to look at and change in ourselves. Psychology calls this behavior "projection."

For example, let's imagine that I don't want to know that I ever behave dishonestly, because I value honesty and believe I try hard to be honest and am an honest person. My dishonesty may be so disguised from me that I cannot identify it. If my partner sees it and tries to tell me, but I refuse to hear it or take in his words as true about the ways he sees me being dishonest,

1) I lose the opportunity to observe and change my behaviors,
2) I continue with the hurtful defensive behaviors,

3)   Those behaviors distance me from my partner and others, and

4)   I accuse others of hurting me with those very behaviors.

In other words, what I refuse to see and know about in me, I will hurt other people with, then accuse them of hurting me with those very same behaviors. That is the definition of projection, and we all do it.

That internal picture-show again. The "movie" that runs on our personal internal projector is often about all our unresolved issues from childhood, and the negative traits from those unresolved issues are what we project onto others and accuse them of doing to us. The principle of projection applies especially to our partners. They are our easiest, most likely targets, because aspects of their energy remind our unconscious mind of our primary caregivers in childhood.

Even if we have reviewed our childhood to a great extent, but are still protecting Mom and Dad from being seen as flawed and imperfect, we can be sure that we are *toxic* in our close relationships. Our projector is running a movie onto our loved ones called "All My Old Unresolved Childhood Issues." And we're not even aware it's there!

Cliff and Cindy appeared in therapy because of his constant criticism of her. Cliff was upset with Cindy because she was always so busy with the children, he believed she didn't care about him any more. What this couple discovered as we began to examine their dynamics was that as Cliff felt pushed aside, he criticized Cindy out of his own pain, and Cindy made herself unavailable to Cliff because she felt guilty for being a disappointment to him. Her only success story was with the kids; his only times of feeling really valuable came at work. So this couple had grown apart in order to survive the pain from each other's projector.

As their stories began to unfold, Cliff, the youngest of six children, recounted a childhood of feeling lost in the shuffle among five siblings. He grew up feeling that everything and everybody took precedence over him and his needs. As Cindy distanced from him with the children, he began to feel those old feelings of not being important or even really wanted.

Cindy, on the other hand, the elder of two children, had felt overly responsible to both parents for being the "good" girl, the one who tried hard and helped make their lives better. To Cindy, criticism meant failure. Even thinking she might have disappointed her parents caused her great despair. Cliff's constant criticism and badgering of her kept her feeling like a terrible disappointment to him and that trying to make life better for him was hopeless.

This couple was locked into a downward spiral, neither one getting his or her emotional needs met in the marriage. The hope that things could improve in this relationship grew as Cliff and Cindy came to a broader realization of the way their own parents had dealt with them and how hurtful that had felt. By opening up and exploring their own childhood experiences, they were able to use their knowledge to redirect the way they were dealing with each other in their marriage.

Protecting ourselves. Keeping our parents in the china cabinet also protects *us* to an extent. Idolizing our parents is a form of idolizing ourselves, not owning up to our own flaws and imperfections. You see, if we came from perfect parents, how can *we* be flawed? Once we unveil *their* flaws, we become vulnerable to having *our* flaws exposed as well, even seeing them ourselves for the first time.

This process can be especially threatening for the child who grew up worrying about any flaw of his own, fearing it would cause his parents to reject him. To this child, being less than perfect would bring rejection and the withdrawal of love. The role of having to be perfect might have meant that the child shouldn't:

1) embarrass the parents and make the "family look bad"
2) upset the parents, because they have "enough to deal with"
3) disappoint the parents, because they "try so hard"
4) bother the parents, because they're "too busy to deal with you."

And, in addition to those factors, our parents generally tried to make us believe that they were perfect. I remember working with a client who kept telling me how great her father was, particularly how intelligent.

Finally I asked her, "How did you know he was so smart?"

She thought for a noticeable amount of time, then with ever so slight a grin said, "Well, that's what he always told me."

For some reason parents feel they must encourage the idea that they are perfect, and that message comes across from time to time in one way or another.

Telling it like it is. Adults who are able to jump in and tell their truth about the parenting they got, without *excusing*, *justifying*, *denying*, or *dismissing* it in order to "protect" their parents, are probably furthest along in their journey to becoming emotionally healthy adults.

On the other hand, adults who completely trash their parents and can't seem to find even one redeeming factor about them are probably also hiding from some aspect of truth. Nevertheless, these people are easier to work with and help than the ones who continue to defend and protect their parents. At least the wall is down, the door of the china cabinet is standing wide open, and they can see their parents as human, flawed, and imperfect. Hooray! We can then go to work on discovering how they were wounded as children, and how they now wound others in their present relationships.

Please understand me clearly on this one point: none of the work of therapy or healthy growth is about trashing one's parents.

In fact, trashing one's parents is the flip side of the same coin as idolizing one's parents. The name of that coin is *avoidance.* When we idolize or trash anyone, including our parents, we are avoiding the insights and perspectives necessary to effect change in our own behaviors.

The work is not our parents' to do, it's ours. It's my belief that we need to do this work without our parents even knowing or being involved at any level, except under very special circumstances. Most parents are coming from a background that would never allow them to understand the necessity of doing this work and would probably find it blasphemous. *Idolizing and trashing are two defense tactics that delay our growth and help perpetuate our own ability to wound others, while we continue to live in our denial.* Needing our parents to be perfect or totally unredeemable, either way holds us back from the freedom to experience our full potential.

If you're not ready yet to open the door of your own china cabinet, I hope you'll at least be willing to stand in front of it for a while, look honestly at the images inside, and then decide what would happen if you took the risk of letting in a draft of fresh air.

Chapter 7

Healthy Adult Boundaries

"Where do you end and I begin?"

Our personal boundaries represent a clear definition of our personal space: physically, emotionally, intellectually, sexually, and spiritually. Healthy boundaries separate what's me from what's you, what's mine from what's yours and give others a clear definition of who we are as individual people. Emotionally healthy people have intact, functional boundaries.

Personal boundaries may be physical—for example, the invisible circle that denotes the amount of space we like to have around us when conversing with another person, or the lines of demarcation for areas of our bodies where touches aren't welcome.

Sometimes personal boundaries are emotional—for example, an appropriate respect for another person's privacy or private thoughts, or that invisible line that tells us when another person is taking over too much of what should be our own business.

Our personal boundaries define who we are to ourselves and other people. If we heed them, they let us know when we are being intruded upon by others or excluded by them. Boundaries, working as they should, also let us know when we risk intruding upon others or excluding them.

Communicating our boundaries. Because all relationships have limits, consciously identified or not, it becomes important for us to let others know when we're uncomfortable with the way they interact with us. It's also our responsibility to be sensitive to cues when others are letting us know how we intrude upon or exclude them.

Exchanging this information with one another works if it's done with mutual respect. Only when someone is becoming abusive does the boundary communication break down. Abusers are not usually aware of or use the sensitivity to know when they're violating another person's boundaries, and that unawareness becomes part of how they keep their intimidating power going. *The way someone feels, however awful it may be, never gives that person the right to abuse someone else.* My next two sentences may sound simplistic, but putting them into practice is one of the hardest things some of us ever have to learn to do.

1. *If abuse is happening to me as an adult, it's my responsibility to speak up to the abuser and let him or her know clearly that I'm experiencing their behavior as abusive and will not stay present for more abuse.*

2. *If I am a child being abused, I need to be able to speak up to some trusted adult in my life who will report the abuse and take responsibility for getting it stopped.*

In either case, if I don't speak up, my silence protects the abuser and enables the abusive behavior to go on.

Modifying the old saying just a bit, abuse takes two to tango—one to abuse, one to tolerate the abuse.

When we were kids, other people set our boundaries—parents, teachers, the adults in our lives. The limits they set usually had to do with our personal safety and how we interacted with them and our peers. The adults in charge of our physical and emotional safety were themselves responsible for not violating our boundaries, even though they held the power to do so if they chose. And, tragically, many of them did so choose.

As we grow up, we need to learn the importance of protecting ourselves from violations by others, which we can do by setting our own healthy limits and boundaries. Children who grew up in ideal situations—if such a situation ever exists—had parents who allowed them to experience their own personal power around boundaries. Such children were allowed to say, respectfully, "No" and "Stop" to their parents and anyone else, including other adults, who were hurting them. It's a skill every one of us should have as we start our journey through life, but very few of us learn it until long after we need it, if ever.

The sad truth is that most of us were raised by people who never even heard of a personal boundary and would have taken great exception to a child who tried to tell someone (especially an adult) that she had limits about how she wanted to be treated. Most of us grew up believing that no matter how badly we were treated in our families, or by friends, teachers, and any adults in authority, we were expected simply to endure it.

And if we were good at enduring, we were usually labeled the "good kid." If we weren't good at enduring and fought back, we were usually labeled "the rebel." Only in recent years has our society realized that *even very young children need to learn the concept of healthy personal boundaries, because without them, they won't be able to take care of themselves in life and are at risk for becoming anyone's victim.*

Boundaries, not walls. Boundaries differ from walls in that walls are about keeping others out, separated and disconnected from us, whereas boundaries are about allowing others in while we take care of ourselves as we stay together and connected.

Walls say, "Leave me alone!" or "I'm out of here!" or "You can't treat me that way!" or "How dare you say that, feel that, act that way!"

Boundaries say, "Let's decide a way we can work this out together." "Let me describe to you how I experience your hurtful energy, and you do the same for me." "If you need to talk that way, I want you to understand that I won't try to interfere with it; however, I will take a short break and come back when you feel calmer, and will speak to me with respect."

Actually, a person can talk, feel, and act anyway he or she chooses, as long as that person can get away with it. Who says when enough is enough? It's up to the person *receiving* it to decide their own limits about how much they will stay to hear or tolerate.

A great societal challenge. Teaching children healthy boundaries is one of the biggest needs confronting our society today. It seems that the dysfunctional family is the only family we've got, and dysfunctional families do not understand personal boundaries.

Girls who grow up in households where boundaries are continually violated tend to hook up with boundary-violators when they move into adult relationships with men, becoming victims of domestic abuse themselves and often bringing children into a home where child abuse is a way of life. Boys whose boundaries are continually violated grow up harboring chronic anger toward authority figures and often sabotage their own lives or end up in prison through their misguided efforts to strike back.

If parents model healthy personal boundaries, kids will learn them more quickly and more effectively. Telling someone in words how to ride a bike or drive a stick-shift car is not the best way to help that person learn. It's far more helpful to let them *see you do it*, and then guide them in a positive, encouraging way as they learn to do it competently themselves.

It's the same with boundaries. Parents who have good boundaries and respect the boundaries of their children are teaching quickly and well. This is an essential part of good parenting—teaching kids about healthy personal space by modeling it and allowing kids to experience it themselves.

How not to do it. Let's talk about what might happen in a family's life around anger. Suppose the father, John, becomes angry at his wife June. If John begins yelling, throwing things, calling June names, threatening her, June, depending upon her own life experience and temperament, will probably either retreat and withdraw into silence, or else fight back and throw a few things of her own. If she fights back, she's as irresponsible and regressed as he is, and if she clams up and says nothing, she's disrespecting herself by allowing him to continue abusing her.

Children who watch such scenes are seeing boundaries violated all over the place—physical, emotional, spiritual. Neither parent respects the other's dignity or the other's rights. Neither partner holds the other in any degree of positive regard. And those children, when they grow up and make their own relationships, will probably be withdrawers and yellers, name-callers, and plate-throwers as well—one mess of a family life.

How to do it better. If, on the other hand, John and June understand healthy boundaries, they will *hold the tension of their discomfort*, acknowledge in words that they are upset, take a pause, breathe, set a time to sit down and go over the issue together, problem-solve, and reach a resolution through cooperation that will work for both of them. Although no one is denying his or her anger, these two partners respect one another, treat one another with positive regard, and work together for the good of the relationship and the family's life. What a gift their children will receive in watching them go through this healthy, constructive process! We should all have been so lucky growing up.

Boundaries and our life history. The boundaries we appreciate and need in a relationship have everything to do with our history—not only what we experienced, but how we experienced it. No two persons have the same life experience or reaction to their experience. Even children raised in the same family experience that family differently. So it makes sense that two partners coming into a committed love relationship bring their own distinct histories with them and will see life from very different angles. Thus each partner will have differing expectations around any given boundary issue. That's what we all butt up against when we attempt to have enduring relationships—a partner who sees life through very different eyes, requiring some adjustment on both sides.

If my partner grew up in a household of silent withdrawers, and I grew up in a family of yellers and name-callers, we have some serious work ahead of us in terms of establishing boundaries that will serve. His withdrawal and silence may feel like boundary violations to me, while my name-calling and yelling will certainly feel like boundary violations to him. If we continue practicing the same boundaries or lack of them that we experienced in our families of origin, our marriage is not going to make it in the long run.

No two partners ever come to a committed love relationship with identical boundary expectations, and every couple must expect to work to establish boundaries that serve to keep their relationship emotionally safe.

Changing the delivery system. *Most of the time in relationships, we don't have to change who we are or our opinions and beliefs. We only have to be willing to change our delivery – our communication – of who we are, our opinions and beliefs.*

To make the relationship work, my partner will need to be willing to teach me how he or she wants me to deliver my beliefs and opinions to him or her, and vice versa. Most of the time we can hear the *content* of what our partner is trying to tell us. It is their *delivery* that alerts our defenses and makes it difficult, if not impossible, to hear what is being said. If partners can learn to say, "I'm not having difficulty hearing the *content* of what you are trying to tell me. It's your *delivery* that I experience as disrespectful and hurtful. Here is how I would prefer you to give me this information:_____" And it becomes that person's job to fill in the blanks for the other on how better he or she might hear what is being said.

A relationship doesn't work well when one partner expects the other to be a mind-reading expert, nor does it work satisfactorily unless both partners are willing to teach each other who they are and how they want to be treated in the relationship.

We must both be willing to learn how our partners want us to *alter our delivery,* and we must both be willing to teach our partners how we want them to handle or communicate with us. This is really the essence of healthy relationships—*two people willing to learn their own needs and wants and then express those needs and wants to their partners in an effective, non-wounding way, so that their connection isn't broken.*

If you have been gentle and appropriate in your delivery or expression, what your partner will do with this information has everything to do with the partner and his or her history. It has nothing to do with you. *It's important to recognize that the partner always has a choice of how to respond.* He or she may try to help you get your needs met, or he or she may refuse to help you meet them. A positive response or a negative one is your partner's choice, not a personal rejection of you. And you have no control over that choice.

We are in charge of efforts, but we're not in charge of outcomes. Our goal should always be serving the good of the relationship, and mutually satisfying relationships depend upon the input and positive effort of both partners in it. Our personal responsibility lies in learning to *say out loud* to our partner what we are not liking about the way he or she treats us in the relationship, then going on to say what it is that we would like.

For example, when Rob and Ruth first began dating, she had trouble talking about highly charged personal issues. Ruth had grown up in a family where such issues were dealt with by ignoring unpleasant facts, refusing to discuss them, hanging up in the middle of telephone conversations, or hastily fleeing the room to sulk. Rob had grown up in a family that would bring highly charged matters into the open to be talked through, even if things got loud and disrespectful. So conflicts were bound to arise if these two young people stayed in relationship.

While they were dating, the first few times Ruth hung up the phone, Rob told her that he was not comfortable with this reaction, and what he wanted from her was to be willing to sit with her discomfort long enough for them to talk about it. He said if she continued with the hanging-up response he wouldn't want to stay in the relationship, and Ruth heard what he said and stopped hanging up.

When Rob expressed his disdain for her family's way of dealing with things, Ruth felt put down, and eventually she had to tell him so and ask that he not speak derisively of her family any more, no matter what he thought of their methods. She was learning a better way of dealing with conflict, because she loved Rob and was willing to try something new, and because Rob loved her too, he was willing to teach her a method that produced better results in their partnership, and he was open to learn from her how to alter his own hurtful behaviors.

Now that Rob and Ruth are married and have a little girl, the way conflict is handled in their household is setting a great example for their daughter, who will grow up with healthy, intact personal boundaries and solution-based patterns for dealing with conflict in her own relationships.

Mind-reading and silence won't fix anything. If I continue in my learned pattern of expecting a partner to read my mind, I'm automatically setting up my partner and the relationship to fail, because no one can read another person's mind.

If you don't tell me what's bothering you, but I see you continuing all day with a sulky expression on your face, banging things around in the workshop or the kitchen, slamming doors or sitting staring gloomily into space, I don't know whether your feet hurt or you're mad because I forgot to do something you asked. And I *never* will know unless I *ask* you, and you *tell* me.

When it's obvious to me something's bothering you, and I ask, "Honey, what's wrong?" absolutely the least helpful and most annoying answer you can give is, "Oh, nothing. Nothing's wrong." By refusing to admit something's bothering you, you're implying that I'm either a nitwit or crazy for assuming something is bothering you. Then I feel even less valued than I felt before, when you weren't letting me in on the cause of your unease, and the relationship is in a worse place than it was at the start.

Address the behavior, not the person. We need to pay attention to any behavior coming from our partner that we don't like and are not addressing. Some annoying or any hurtful behaviors we allow to continue and protect with our silence only builds resentment. If your partner speaks to you too loudly, gruffly, sarcastically, or in a demeaning manner, unless you address the fact right there while it is happening—according to a pre-discussed and agreed-upon plan—you're sending the message that speaking to you in that manner is okay and you will tolerate it. Furthermore, by your silence you're *protecting* your partner from having to make any changes about the way he speaks to you.

Often my clients tell me, "Why should I say anything? It will just make my partner madder, and I know he's not going to change anyway!"

Let's be clear. The purpose of speaking up is not to change the other person. If that should happen, it's a bonus and a choice that is totally up to your partner. The speaking up is for ourselves, our own boundaries, not our partner. Once we've reported the behavior that's making us uncomfortable, even though we can't control what our partner does with that information, we're taking responsibility for ourselves, making our own truth clear, and moving out of the Victim Box (see Chapter 10).

Let's suppose Judy's partner Jeff belittles and blames her, and Judy tells him she doesn't appreciate it, and asks him to speak to her with respect. If Jeff tries to honor Judy's request by speaking respectfully to her, Judy is willing to stay present with Jeff—Plan A— and hear what he has to say. But if Jeff refuses, his refusal places the ball back in Judy's court.

Then Judy has a decision to make. How much disrespectful treatment is she willing to be available for and tolerate? Imagine that this couple has danced to this same tune many times in their marriage, and that at a time when conflict wasn't present, they sat down and designed a Plan B *together*, so they would have a place to go if Plan A didn't work. Here's what they agreed upon:

1. Judy tells Jeff how he talks and acts with her that she doesn't like: "It feels disrespectful to me when you use sarcasm or criticize my character as a person." Jeff mirrors and validates her words unconditionally.

2. Judy tells Jeff how she wants him to talk and act with her instead of how he is doing it: "I want you to speak to me with a calm voice, medium volume, soft facial features (especially around your mouth), and describe what I have done to upset you without making reference to my character." Jeff mirrors and validates her words unconditionally.

3. If Jeff agrees, he comes up with a way that Judy can remind or *guide* him back on track if he runs off the road with their Plan B, which he will. (Absolutely none of us can resort to this new, healthy behavior without messing up many, many times before we are conscious enough to do it as planned.) Jeff asks her to say in a soft, calm voice, "Jeff, do you want a minute to start over?" That will be his cue that he needs to stop and regroup and begin again.

When energies get too high and things cannot continue because of the heat of the moment, this couple could even make up a Plan C that might sound like this:

Jeff and Judy agree that either partner can say, "Let's take a fifteen-minute pause. After that, I'll come back and bring up this same topic, and we can try again to discuss it, and if that doesn't work, we'll continue with the pauses until we can reach some resolution to the issue."

These trials may take two or three days (or weeks) in the beginning; however, if they stick with it, Judy and Jeff are slowly *building the belief system* that they can resolve issues in ways that don't have to redamage either partner (see Chapter 3 for details on how to work out a plan for when things get too heated for comfort).

Here's my rule for postponing any discussion, which I call the "Return and Reinitiate Rule": *The partner who postpones any discussion carries the entire burden at that moment for saying when and where the discussion will pick up again, plus that same person must arrive at the appointed place first and reinitiate the topic.*

Telling my partner my plan of action is something I must do at a time when neither of us is mad or upset, and I will invite my partner's ideas into the plan, so that it becomes "our" plan. If my partner resists working with me on a plan, I need to calmly tell my partner the plan and make it clear that this is something I will do for me and my personal sense of emotional safety in our relationship.

State your boundaries, but give up the idea that you can control outcomes. Remember, by approaching conflict in this way, you are not trying to control your partner. *None of us can control another person, unless we are holding that person hostage, and even then we can't control what he says, does, thinks, or feels at any given moment.* Once I've set my boundary, my partner can then go on talking however he or she chooses, for as long as he or she likes. The difference is that, if it remains hurtful, I will not be present to see and hear it. I am setting limits for what I will tolerate, and my partner can set his or her own, or, hopefully, we can set them together as a "we" solution for when we violate each others personal boundaries—which we will, if we remain alive and together.

Suppose we're talking about Anthony and his wife Anita. Anthony has a short fuse and is quick to squelch any outburst, except his own. Even though he claims to want peace and harmony in his home, his comments to Anita and the children are sharp criticisms, punctuated with shaming slurs. Not surprisingly, he was brought up in a household where his father behaved the same way. Now Anthony bombards his wife and kids with words. His voice is booming, with an unpleasant edge. He criticizes, blames, and belittles his wife. He rages at and demeans his kids.

Anita hates this aspect of her family life, and most of the respect or affection she ever felt for Anthony is gone. But she feels trapped, because she grew up in a family where—guess what—her mother was treated the same way, and her mother, like Anita, was taught that the wife's role was to *endure*.

When Anita complained to her mother about Anthony's treatment, Mom told her, "Anita, this is life. Grow up and make the best of it. Anthony has never hit you, and he works hard to provide."

Anita has been trying to make the best of it, but nothing changes. She just feels worse and worse, and she believes that anything she says to Anthony will only make him explode more. Plus, now, she feels some guilt because her mother expects her to tolerate his inappropriateness and count her blessings, since he has never hit her.

What do you suppose Anthony thinks about all of this? He believes that their family life is normal, and because Anita never complains or tells him to stop, she must approve of his behavior. He would be shocked to know that Anita isn't happy with their life. The life he has with Anita and the kids is very much like the home he grew up in, so to Anthony that feels normal. He behaves like his father, and Anita behaves a lot like his mother. Anthony's thoughts on the subject certainly don't match up with Anita's.

But Anita has allowed his unacceptable behavior to continue by not addressing it, and she continues to send the message that it is okay to treat her and the kids this way. She has let her own boundaries be violated, and does not protect the boundaries of her children.

Now, suppose Anita reads a book about dealing with boundary abuse, and she decides to try to make a change in the situation. This takes a lot of courage on Anita's part, but she's heard the saying, "If nothing changes, nothing changes." And what she really wants is a better, happier life. So she gets all her courage up, figures out what her Plan B might be, feeds Anthony a big supper with a special dessert, brings him in a cup of coffee, and sits down to tell him.

"Anthony, I've made up my mind I won't accept the way you talk to me any more," she says. "I expect you to start speaking to me with respect." She's scared to death saying it, but she's taking responsibility for herself at last.

Anthony is amazed. She's never complained before. So he blows off her complaint: "That's just the way I am. My dad was that way, and that's the way I am, too."

Now Anita has a choice to make. Yes, Anthony has a family history of boundary violations, and she had the same history in her own family. But she's decided that it's time to break the cycle. Anita knows that she doesn't like to be talked to in that manner, and she wants it to stop. If she doesn't tell Anthony clearly how she wants to be talked to, no one else will do it for her.

Still clinging to her courage, she makes her point again, quietly. "I was serious about what I said, Anthony. If you have something to say to me, even if you're upset, I'll appreciate it if you keep your voice at a medium level, be calm, and use words that tell me exactly what the problem is without hurtful and degrading remarks to me or the kids."

Anthony doesn't know where this new woman is coming from, and he doesn't know how to handle it. So he keeps up the bluster. "Huh! If I have to talk like that, it's no use for me to even talk at all!"

Anita has given him a choice: honor her request to change his delivery, or refuse to change. So far it looks as if he's refusing to change, so Anita may have to move on to Plan B. Once again, it's up to her to take care of herself and set some limits for what she will tolerate and what she will subject her children to.

She's already been working on Plan B, so her response is ready. In the calmest, softest voice she can manage, she says, "When your voice gets loud and your words criticize me, shame me, or belittle me, I will tell you calmly that I'm taking a fifteen-minute pause, then come back and try to have a more respectful discussion. If you are not calmer in fifteen minutes, we can take another brief pause, or we can try again at a time that you suggest. We can work together on this as long as we need to, so we can stay connected while you give me your information in a respectful way."

Unless she says these words in a calm manner when they are in conflict, she could easily send a punishing message that Anthony may interpret this way: "If you don't speak to me the way I want to be spoken to, I'm out of here!" But she isn't at that point yet, and if she makes that mistake, speaking angrily and seeming to make threats, her inappropriateness matches his, and they've made no progress whatsoever in hearing each others' reality on their issue of conflict.

Anita is on the right track. She and Anthony both needed some education about healthy, connected relationships, and luckily they got it. Even though Anita was mad at Anthony for the way he treated her, she was not only allowing it, but encouraging it by not addressing it. *One partner is not "getting away" with any behavior that the other partner will no longer tolerate.* It was just as hard for Anita to grow into setting and holding healthy boundaries as it was for Anthony to grow into containing and appropriately addressing his frustrations. Both had to go against the way they had been taught to deal with their feelings. Both had to stretch into new territory to resolve these problems. Both are learning to move into the "we" connection of long-term committed love relationships.

We're partners, not parents. Even though in terms of years we're adult human beings, we often deal with our partners as if one of us is the parent and one is the child. Many relationships go on for years with one partner or the other maintaining the majority of power, so that the "child" partner feels powerless, resentful, and often angry, and the "parent" partner feels in control of the relationship. We call these "parenting relationships." They are not healthy partnerships for adults, and they are not satisfying for either partner.

In partner relationships, all of us want to be treated as equals, with neither partner holding a majority of the power. Ideally, the power flows back and forth between both partners. *Partnering is not parenting, because in true partnering both partners share the power of expressing their needs and wants, and help each other get those needs and wants met,* within the limits of the partners' capabilities.

Look for partnering solutions. In order to find solutions that work for the good of our relationships, we need to forget about parenting solutions, which work primarily to the benefit of the "parent"—the person holding most of the authority and power. The far more satisfying alternative is a partnering solution, which works for both partners, with both partners sharing the power and responsibility of their relationship.

In a situation where we have no personal power, or believe our personal power is limited, the struggle to try to set personal limits and boundaries demands a great deal of energy. Most of us have grown up without being given permission to even have boundaries, so that when we first begin to try to set them, we are often too aggressive about it and go overboard.

When boundaries are overlooked. Most of us arrive at age 18 with little or no permission to take care of ourselves emotionally and maybe even physically, because for the previous eighteen years our welfare was in the hands of people who had no concept of the need or even the existence of personal boundaries or limits. Somebody was always there to say, "You can," or "You can't," and when we asked why, the answer was, "Because I said so." Rarely does anyone say, "You're entitled to have your boundaries respected, and I'm going to help you set safe ones."

Having personal boundaries means claiming our personal power, moving out of the Victim Box, taking responsibility for our lives. It means we understand that we all have the right to stand up for ourselves and the responsibility to speak our truths, especially in close relationships. And who can set these boundaries and ask that they be respected? Only the person who needs them. Setting boundaries and asking that they be honored is one of the important tasks of healthy living with other people.

When a partner doesn't want boundaries. Sometimes a partner does not want the other partner to have boundaries. Right away that's a red flag for the relationship. If one partner considers boundaries a threat to the relationship, it's a pretty reliable signal that this person has learned to survive by dominating and controlling others.

Let's suppose Timothy doesn't want his partner Tiffany to have boundaries, because he knows that if she has them, he won't be in full control of the relationship. When Tiffany realizes this, she will need to address this problem with Timothy. If he isn't willing to listen, *hold the tension of his discomfort*, and allow Tiffany to *help him alter this dominating behavior*, Tiffany will have a decision to make about whether or not to pursue this relationship. Timothy will need to look at his fear around losing control. What is that about in his history? How does Tiffany scare him about control? If he can open up, explore these areas, and share this information with Tiffany, this couple can probably work through these control issues. Because Tiffany has her own control agenda going, which needs to be discovered and altered as well, Timothy will need to help her identify and alter her defenses around control. Then both partners can move into sharing the power of their relationship. This is a mutual process necessary for *differentiation*. (See Chapter 8 on Stages)

Why we want to control. All of us are trying to control the space that we occupy on this planet, not because we are control freaks, or have a desperate need to dominate everything in our life. *We are all controlling out of fear*, because our Old Brain vividly remembers what life was like for us as children when we had no control. That reactive part of us, our Old Brain or Unconscious Mind, is trying to prevent that old scenario from happening again in our adult relationships.

The threat of change. Whenever a relationship changes in any way, that change can feel threatening. Most of us resist change until we can experience that the change will be for the better, and even then we usually find going through the change hard. We all fear the unknown more than the known. Frequently when one person in a relationship goes through a significant personal change of some kind, the other person in the relationship may become uncomfortable with that change and in fact may even leave the relationship. Healthy relationships thrive on mutual personal growth, and even if one partner feels threatened by limits and boundaries, that uncomfortable partner still has no right to dictate to or pressure the other to remain at an immature, infantile stage of emotional development.

Partners who demand it all their way. Another red flag for relational problems is a partner or even a friend who wants to isolate you from other friends and, especially, from your family. Of course, if your family is so unhealthy that it makes you unhealthy too, this is a different concern. Abusive families need to be isolated from the ones they have abused until the abuse is permanently stopped. Partners who want to isolate you from the rest of the world are very insecure and feel threatened unless you make them the center of your world. And with many insecure people, even being the center of your world is never enough.

Other undesirable partners. Red-flag people come in many flavors.

- Those with bad tempers who expect you to tolerate them
- Those who feel entitled to treat you any way they like and expect you to tolerate it
- Those who expect you to do all the work of the relationship (go to therapy, pay for therapy, read the books, learn the skills, and "fix" the relationship, which in their terms usually means "fixing" yourself)
- Those who refuse to honor your limits or boundaries or even be told "No."

All of the above partners will insist on relationships without healthy boundaries, because the red-flag, *undifferentiated* partner needs to be in full charge of the relationship, which won't allow the space necessary for healthy mutual boundaries. More often than not, relationships with the red-flag, *undifferentiated* partners mentioned above include the toxic element of one or more of the four chemical addictions: alcohol, drugs, food, and sex (see Chapter 9 for a more detailed discussion of addictions).

Summing up. Let's assume that a relationship begins with two willing adults who want to partner, not parent. Both want the relationship, both want it to be healthy. In order for that to happen, they have to travel a two-way street. Each partner must

- *Ask the other to say specifically how he or she wants to be treated in the relationship.*
- *Tell the other specifically how he or she wants to be treated in the relationship.*

Never assume that we know what our partner wants, nor assume that our partner knows what we want. Neither of us is a mind-reader. We will both be learning where one of us starts and the other stops, and vice versa. Boundaries are essential, and the skills necessary for building them are not hard to learn. Keep it simple!

Learn to tell your partner:

If both partners follow the plan laid out for Judy and Jeff, they will begin to *build the belief system* that they can *hold the emotional connection safe* in their relationship while they work through their differences. Children in the family will learn appropriate methods for establishing personal space, addressing conflict, and learning to value their own different selves as they allow others to do the same. *Differentiation* of the entire family can be the positive result of this work. (Refer to Chapter 8 for differentiation.)

One last piece about boundaries. Whether anyone else does or does not have boundaries does not determine whether you can have boundaries. You make that decision yourself. *You are never at the mercy of anyone who refuses to honor your boundaries, unless you are a dependent child or an adult who is making the choice to be in that position.* Boundaries are the result of choices and conscious, intentional behavior. Boundaries make for healthy relationships and happier people.

Chapter 8

Matching Up the Stages

"Well, you're acting like a two-year-old!"

Romantic Love is the first stage of a committed love relationship. It begins with an initial attraction to a potential partner. If the attraction "takes" and a relationship is formed, several powerful things begin to happen that are unique to the Romantic Love Stage.

A chemical high. The first occurrence is a sudden overproduction of chemicals produced in both partners' brains, called *endorphins*, that anesthetize the new lovers. Hard to imagine love as anesthesia, but that's how it works. In the natural course of any day, all human brains produce these morphine-like chemicals, but nothing like the immense amounts of them that flood our brains in Romantic Love.

Part of endorphins' normal function is to reduce our awareness of every little pain we might encounter throughout the day. During Romantic Love, these endorphins are pumped out in greatly increased amounts and keep us numbed to negative, upsetting feelings our new love interest may stir up. Therefore, since our ever-vigilant Old Brain has blocked out all awareness of our new partner's negative qualities, we perceive the chosen one as basically perfect and excuse everything imperfect about him or her.

The marriage movie. The second thing happening in Romantic Love is a "movie" that begins running in each partner's brain, an ideal image that is projected out onto the potential partner. The title of this movie is "My Definition of Love." It includes any and all pieces that make up the individual person's own definition of love, based in his or her own reality. Every time one partner looks into the other's face, all that partner can see is his or her own unique and highly satisfying definition of love. And we all know how good that feels!

"I am the greatest." Another very powerful feature that comes with Romantic Love is the enormous attraction we feel to a partner when we perceive that the other person finds us extremely attractive and entirely lovable. The new love interest helps us believe that we *are* truly wonderful. And who doesn't like that!

This perception of being found attractive and desirable is the fuel that drives affairs. If I meet someone who thinks I'm wonderful, naturally that feels so much better than being with my present partner, who thinks I'm terrible. Of course, the new flame has never lived with me in a committed love relationship, so I can *make up a story* of how life could be with the two of us together—my new partner adoring me forever. And then the affair is off and running, until reality sets in. Romantic Love sets up an artificial drug-induced state that allows partners to believe they can securely and reliably attach to one another and trust each other totally, without anybody ever getting hurt.

Romantic Love equals Attachment stage. This stage of Romantic Love mimics the very first task of a newborn baby in its emotional development—Attachment. In Attachment, the baby's developmental task is to become firmly and securely *attached* to at least one primary caregiver. This connected state with our primary caregiver feels safe, content, and the source of life for us as babies. Similarly, two people in Romantic Love experience the same high level of emotional safety and trust. Lovers tend to isolate from the world in order to be fully focused on and attached to each other. They tell deeply hidden secrets and empty their hearts and souls to their beloved, with all the trust and dependency of a newborn. Like the baby and its primary caregiver, the lovers recognize one another as their lifeline and are mutually mesmerized.

This incredibly high level of trust in another person, without reservations, is achieved only because of the artificial, euphoric, chemically induced trance of lovers and harks back to the necessary dependency of a newborn. Ordinarily those are the only two times in our lives—when we're newly born and when we are in Romantic Love—when we're able to trust another person so unconditionally.

Being in love is a unique and delightful period of life. We want and expect it to last forever. Yet during this time we are truly not in our right minds and don't always make the best decisions for our lives. In Romantic Love you hear each partner describe his or her new love interest with the very words that are scripted in that individual's projected movie, *e.g.*, "thoughtful, great sense of humor, sensitive, extremely intelligent, caring, loving," etc.

During this period, couples are focused on how *alike* they are, and you hear them express this: "We like the same books, music, foods, colors, actors, games," and so on and so on, *ad nauseam*. They will also tell you that their unlike qualities make for "delightful differences that keep everything interesting." Amazing.

So, during this initial stage, with the help of the *endorphins* and the *positive movie* each partner is running, the couple remains in a euphoric state within the relationship. During this time of protective numbing provided by the endorphins, the new lovers do and accept things they will be unable to do or accept later on, after the endorphins have worn off and their positive movies have stopped running. It's as if they have both been high on the elixir of love, until one day the elixir of love isn't being produced any more, and then the hangover comes.

Once we understand how powerful this state is for all of us, it's not hard to see, then, why we will commit to a partner, get married, and make it permanent. We think we're committing to the euphoric state forever and ever. And why not? Wouldn't that be just wonderful?

The Power Struggle. The truth is, though, that we are really committing to move to the next predictable stage of a primary love relationship, called the Power Struggle. The Power Struggle usually creeps in without our full awareness. The endorphins are slowing down to a normal dose, and our positive love-movie slows to a halt. The language of *disillusionment* creeps in as we begin to change our complimentary opinion of our partner to a critical one. Instead of talking about how *alike* we are, we begin to notice how *different* we are. We will say, usually in anger, "I never knew you were that way!" or "You sound just like my mother (or father)!" We talk about how we don't really have that much in common any more, and some of us now claim we *never* had much in common. We believe we have just "grown apart." None of this is true; we convince ourselves that it is, however, and blame our partners for tricking us or hiding their faults.

The Horror Show. Actually, the only thing that has changed is that we have moved to the second stage of a primary love relationship—the Power Struggle. The endorphins are back to normal levels, so the euphoria is gone, and our positive movie has been replaced with a horror show entitled, "Everything I Have Ever Dreaded Happening To Me In A Close Relationship."

Partners are *disillusioned*. Each quickly begins to *rewrite their history* with the other so that they can leave the marriage with less guilt. What might once have been described as the luckiest day of our life—meeting our beloved—is now viewed as that fateful time in our life that caused us to meet and marry the "wrong" person. We may tell ourselves and anybody else who will listen that we only married our partner so that we could "leave home and get a new start in life," or because we got "caught up in the moment and said yes." The dream marriage we bargained for has become a nightmare, and the very traits we first admired that drew us to our partner are now the qualities about that person that upset us the most!

How it plays out. For example, Chatty Cathie, the more socially adept one in the partnership, was first viewed by her bridegroom Silent Sam as "terrifically outgoing, admired by everyone for her congenial personality and ability to talk to anyone in almost any situation." But now in Sam's eyes she is "disruptive, always having to have the spotlight, never able to shut up."

And Cathie, who first saw Sam as "quiet, thoughtful, maybe a little shy, but strong and deep of spirit" now complains that he's "unable to communicate, withdrawn, completely lacking in spirit."

This is a typical example of how the Power Struggle plays out, and if partners are not aware of what is happening, the marriage could easily end here. But the marriage doesn't have to end, if the two partners understand that *the Power Struggle is supposed to happen*, just as Romantic Love is supposed to happen. It's part of the process. Both stages have a purpose that promotes the potential growth and enduring quality of the relationship, and both stages are supposed to end.

When Romantic Love ends, the couple believes they have "fallen out of love." When the Power Struggle begins, the couple is sure the relationship cannot survive, or, if it does, they don't want to be there to live it. If couples can *hold the tension of their discomfort*, however, and begin working through their conflict, they can move into the very relationship they wanted from the beginning when they first "fell in love."

Power Struggle = Childhood Exploration and Identity. In a committed love relationship, the Power Struggle actually replicates two other stages of childhood emotional development, the Stages of Exploration and Identity, which normally begin around 18 months of age and persist through about 4 years of age.

Now, why would we want to study and understand these stages? We need to do it because they can help us identify those parts of ourselves that are still unfinished from childhood, which become grist for the mill during the adult Power Struggle. Everything we are as adults is rooted in our childhood experience.

It is during this time that the healthy child in an emotionally healthy family is moving from total dependence upon and constant attachment to the primary caregiver into a new need for independent maneuvering. The child's intensely focused world is now opening up. By 18 months, the child is walking and gaining an increased interest as all his senses lure him into the bigger world—its smells, textures, colors, tastes, etc. While the child still wants his caregiver nearby for safety and security, he also clamors for the independence to practice his newfound skills of mobility and language.

As the child moves through these two stages, if encouraged and kept safe enough, she will have gained a significant amount of independence and come to understand that she is indeed a unique person separate from the primary caregiver. Unless something hinders it, children recognize during this period that they are not an extension of their primary caregiver, nor are they permanently attached to anyone. At this stage of life the child's natural task is to begin to develop its own identity in order to become an individual, separate and unique from anyone else on this earth.

Differentiation matters. This process, called *differentiation*, is a necessary part of healthy development that begins to emerge during the stages of Exploration and Identity. *Differentiation* happens as the child develops and recognizes his own separate uniqueness as a person. Yet very few of us were able to experience it as nature intended it to work. Why? Because our parents were coming from an era when encouraging or even allowing children to think independently and act without permission was considered neglectful parenting. Our parents insisted that we see life through *their* eyes and operate as if we had *their* reality, instead of a separate one of our own.

Those of us who were not allowed to differentiate from our caregivers, during the ages from 2 to 4 years, feel threatened when others, especially our partners, try to be, think, and act differently from us. We believe that we have the only *right* reality, just as our parents taught us that they held the only *real* truth, and it becomes our mission to convince others of *our* reality and rebel against *theirs*. Without even trying, we have become our own parents.

In adult committed love relationships, this long-overdue process of trying to *differentiate* ourselves from another loved human being becomes the adult Power Struggle. It begins when one partner, or both, feels safe enough or stifled enough in the relationship to explore their separate identities and existence outside the relationship as well as within it.

Hanging in there. *The growth opportunity the Power Struggle offers is about learning to be in a committed love relationship and holding onto one's uniqueness, while remaining connected to the partner.* There is a definite art to making this passage successfully—from a child who was given no choice but to lose himself in the relationship with the primary caregiver, to an adult able to hold onto his *own* identity while retaining the connection with his life partner. In early days the child's survival depended on his caregiver's winning the Power Struggle. Now, the conquered child who's become an adult struggles against his partner to gain his individuality. Unless this necessary growth is allowed to happen within the adult relationship between partners, the Power Struggle becomes a constant *challenge to win*.

The severity of the adult Power Struggle will depend upon the amount of damage done to the child during those early stages of emotional development. To what extent was the child allowed to differentiate in those early years? Did the child always have to see life through his or her caregiver's eyes? How enmeshed did the child become in trying to be an individual? How much separation was the child allowed to experience while feeling trust that the caregiver was still there? The answers to these questions will be strongly predictive of how much energy and urgency goes into the adult Power Struggle.

Attachment with fear. Another dynamic that surfaces during the adult Power Struggle is a carryover from the Attachment Stage. Kids who had to try to *attach* to caregivers whom they perceived as scary come into adult love relationships with a skewed version of attachment. Fear adds a new energy to any situation. I've observed that the more fear there was in the home where kids were trying to stay attached and grow up, the more fear they bring to adult love relationships in their efforts to attach to one partner. The only kind of attachment they know—the kind they learned in childhood—is *attachment with fear*, yet they don't recognize this as strange, because that's how it was back home.

Without any conscious intention of doing so, they introduce fear into the adult love relationship—either fear of their own or fear engendered in the chosen partner—because that feels like attachment to them. Amazingly, they don't consider their fear defenses—withdrawing, yelling, depression, unavailability, or silent anger—scary or abnormal, because that's what they saw and learned growing up.

Parent power isn't partner power. The adult Power Struggle has a central theme—each partner's efforts to convince the other that there is just *one true reality*, his or hers, and therefore life must proceed along that one "valid" path. Partners will expend tremendous energy disparaging and invalidating the other's reality in an effort to extinguish it:

"You don't know what you are talking about!" or

"Who do you think you are, saying that or doing that?" or

"This is the way it's going to be, and that's that!" or

"I can't depend on you for anything!"

These critical comments invariably sound like a parent belittling a child. This is the point at which partners quit *partnering* and begin attempting to *parent,* in hopes of gaining the power position in the relationship (for a clearer idea of the power position see Chapter 7).

The Power Struggle is named that, of course, because it's about one or the other partner's efforts to *win the power* in the relationship. So long as this effort to sustain a constant power differential continues, the relationship plays out as a parent/child relationship, with one partner always in the power role of parent and the other partner in the powerless role as the child. These roles can switch back and forth from time to time, but unless both partners learn what is actually happening and work together to build the relationship they want, the power differential will remain too great for the partners to stay emotionally connected.

Healthy relationships are not about winning. Mutually satisfying long-term relationships are about connecting emotionally and holding that connection. And we can only get connected and stay connected as adult partners by moving out of that childlike, powerful/powerless set-up. Learning to do this is just one of the skills—the *Foundation Stones*—that go into making a long-term relationship work.

Life offers us no better arena for becoming our best, most grown-up, evolved selves than a committed love relationship, in which both partners have learned how to stay connected while they work their way through their struggles and differences and reap the lifetime rewards true connection brings. In all likelihood we're never completely done with the Power Struggle, because of our strong, basic need to feel unique and special. "Doing" relationships will seem easier if we recognize that the first Power Struggle isn't the last. It will crop up again and again over the long haul, focused on this issue or that. The challenge is to learn to work with the energy arising from our need to differentiate, so that we can arrive at some form of resolution that works for both partners and remain connected as we move into new horizons.

Working without a net. In our society, when the flying-high rush of Romantic Love is gone, we don't feel "in love" any more. At first we were on a free ride of endorphins, positive projections, and complete enmeshment with our partner, and now the ride has wound down. The next time we get this ride will come because both partners have made a *solid commitment* to the relationship and are *working* to stay connected as they live the relationship, without the extra boost of chemicals (endorphins), a love-movie running (our positive projections), or being wrapped up tightly in each other with no boundaries (enmeshment). Then comes the greater thrill, because the relationship is now reality-based and can withstand the perils of real life without driving us to disconnect by numbing out or leaving.

I call this kind of relationship growth *"learning to work without a net,"* and it's not nearly as scary at it sounds. "The net" is our old reactivity, those learned, counterproductive, knee-jerk defenses against the frustration we feel when the endorphins quit flowing, our love-movie stops, the enmeshment ends, and we actually feel our pain with each other. Learning to work without a net means choosing not to react, give up, withdraw, or fall back into our old comfortable knee jerks , in order that we may experience the freedom and greater richness of an authentic, connected, committed relationship.

What it takes to grow. The growth work of the Power Struggle begins moving toward success when couples realize they must hold their own energy safe—not react—for the sake of keeping the connection in the relationship. Doing so requires us to go against our natural instinct to run, hide, attack, yell, or shut down—however our knee-jerk defenses operate.

Just by definition, work means the effort exerted against an opposing force. You may remember from your physics class, a truck traveling a level or downhill road isn't doing work. If it's traveling uphill, however, we define that effort of moving forward against an opposing force—gravity—as work, as the equations below suggest.

Romantic Love = Moving on a level or downhill plane feels natural = No Work

Power Struggle = Moving uphill to stretch into new behaviors and growth = Work

Making a commitment to do this work will lead to a *love that works*! You may refer back to Chapter 4 on Emotional Safety to get clarity on the work necessary to hold the connection with your partner.

Chapter 9

Addictions

"If you really loved me, you'd stop doing that!"

Addictions play a major role in all of our lives, whether we realize it or not. The alcoholic professional, the spendthrift spouse, the workaholic executive, the compulsive womanizer, the anorexic, the batterer —all of these are addicts who adversely affect the lives of those they come in contact with. It was once thought that every alcoholic affects the lives of at least 22 other people. We know now that number is much larger, more like three times 22! Do you see how massive this problem of addictions is in our society?

I frequently work with couples and families mired in addictions. Neither the "problem person" nor the rest of the family is educated about the entire picture of addictions, so they are caught up in a chaotic life, unaware that addictions are the primary reason for the misery and craziness in their lives. Addictions block us from working on any other problems. You see, when we humans are in our right minds, we are normally reachable and teachable. When our brain chemistry is messed up, we are neither.

Human relationships are stressful, and addictions are the primary way Americans cope with stress. Some understanding of addictions is essential, therefore, to help us recognize how profoundly they damage our relationships.

People who rely on addictions to help them cope with life do great damage to those they love or come in contact with, often without realizing it, and even those affected by others' addictions rarely identify addictions as the true cause of the pain.

What constitutes an addiction? In former times, the word "addiction" was applied only to dependence on mind-altering drugs. Today we have a broader understanding of the term. *Anything we use to distract ourselves from facing or dealing with unpleasant feelings can be an addiction.*

Addictions distract us from our pain, redirecting our available energy to *things*, instead of people. Even if our addiction is to a person, the fact that we use that person to soothe ourselves instead of addressing our problems places that person in the category of a thing, rather than a person. Anything we *use* becomes a thing.

On the basis of that definition, *an addiction can center around alcohol or other drugs, food, sex, work, rage, kids, possessions, money (including gambling, debting, or shopping), our partner, religion, physical illness, and numerous other ways we use to distract ourselves.* Addictions are about avoiding emotional pain—the effort to soothe ourselves through some unnatural practice, instead of addressing our emotional pain.

Feeling no pain. We often hear it said of someone who's intoxicated, "He's certainly feeling no pain!" And that's true in more ways than one. Over and above the physical effects of addictions, they're considered *a disease of feelings,* because they kill our real feelings. People who never learn to cope with their feelings often learn to addict to something and consider that an acceptable means of coping with the feelings. We live in a very addictive society, though we don't usually call it that. In our culture, addictive behavior is considered "coping." If we come home tired and stressed, we may reach for a beer or a martini, or use some other chemical to relieve our tiredness and our stress. If we are in conflict with our spouse, we may work, sleep, watch television, shop, drink/drug/smoke, eat, don't eat, get sick often, spend money, have affairs—you can probably add your own ideas to the list.

Why things feel safer than people. Connected, committed relationships between human beings, though they bring great fulfillment, also inevitably bring a certain amount of conflict and misery. Because things don't upset us to the extent people in close relationships do, we find focusing on *things* emotionally safer than focusing on people and close relationships. When we're focusing on things to the extreme of addicting to them, we perceive ourselves as totally in control and in charge of our things. Yet how mistaken that perception is! Anything that becomes an addiction for us will eventually rule our lives, robbing us of the control of our lives, whether we're aware of it or not.

Who is an addict? My theory is that we are *all* addicts in one way or another, and we use our addictions to avoid true intimacy with others, especially our partner and our kids, because that is the closeness that feels the most threatening to us emotionally. To the casual observer, many of the addictions we fall back on can appear admirable—extreme dedication to a job, making a lot of money, staying incredibly thin, always being beautifully groomed and dressed, a lavishly decorated home, doing everything for our children or for others, even when there are many things they need to learn to do for themselves. This is tricky stuff!

We want, even long for the closeness and connection of a loving relationship, but many of us are afraid to take the risk required to let that happen. Growing up in our families of origin, we all experienced enough hurt to feel vulnerable and unsafe. Hence as adults we still feel vulnerable in relationships and sometimes view them as hopeless. It's sad how many people convince themselves, "I'm just not somebody who can be in a relationship." So we fall back on what we see as the reliability of things, instead of making ourselves vulnerable in close but unpredictable human relationships.

Another definition. Pia Mellody has the most accurate definition of addictions I've found:

> An addiction is any process that relieves intolerable reality; and the intensity of that relief is so great that it becomes an increasing priority, taking time and attention away from other priorities, creating consequences that are ignored.

To most of us, the phrase "intolerable reality" means "I'm not happy with my life and the way things are for me," or "I'm not happy inside." This unhappiness can include anything we experience as unpleasant, especially in our most vulnerable area—that's right, relationships. We get emotionally invested in relationships, and when they become uncomfortable or unhappy for us, we don't know what to do to make them better, so they begin to feel intolerable.

When we run from reality. How do addicts relieve "intolerable reality"? We do it by falling back on whatever soothes us and numbs our feelings. When we don't know what else to do to make things right, we see no other choice. Maybe no one ever worked with us or modeled a way for us to deal with unpleasant situations except through some distraction that keeps our emotions numb. Many a parent has distracted a crying child with a lollipop, and we do the same thing in adult life. Only the "lollipops" change!

The phrase "creating consequences that are ignored" is the most descriptive of any addictive behavior. That's the acid test—experiencing painful consequences and continuing the behavior anyway. Addicts can and do vigorously argue against every part of Pia's definition except that final phrase. They can't find a credible or legitimate excuse for the consequences their behaviors create. The proof is in front of their eyes. Creating consequences that are ignored is what happens when the addict refuses to be accountable or responsible for his or her behavior. It's never the addict's fault; he or she always finds someone else to blame: "You drive me to drink! I have to act this way!"

A way for reality to break through. If family members or others close to the addict become willing to stop all rescue attempts and speak up to the addict with honest feedback about the addict's harmful behavior, supplying evidence of the consequences created by the addictive behavior *without watering it down*, the addict often finds this evidence too compelling to refute. That is the goal of an *intervention*—a structured, carefully rehearsed process coordinated by a trained professional, in which a group of concerned persons close to an addict can break through that wall of denial with the goal of finding help.

Unfortunately, families usually don't realize they have this choice until things are at the breaking point. Having endured the addiction and its consequences so long, trying not to upset the addict by mentioning it, they forget that there might be a better way to live. Many of these family members have done the same thing they did in their scary childhood homes—they've "normalized" their misery. Counseling professionals can help with bringing this breakthrough choice to light, educating families how to hold onto their painful realities of the situation and become willing to confront the addict in order to help him or her get sober and sane again.

At the point when concerned others finally give feedback and report evidence that the addict cannot refute, he or she usually responds in one of three ways:

1. Goes into treatment or other recovery work such as Twelve-Step program,
2. Gets furious and shuts the family up with threats or scary behavior, or
3. Acts so pathetic that the family backs down and apologizes, which allows the addict to continue down the same old destructive path.

Addicts don't have to heed what families report to them about those ignored consequences, but the consequences are painfully clear to everyone who's struggling to endure until such time as the addict becomes willing to face the reality of their life. Whether the addict accepts help or not, a degree of relief comes for the rest of the family once they begin openly discussing what's really going on, because they're out from under the painful tension of hiding the family skeleton in the closet.

The impact on families. Some of us are addicted in ways that society applauds. We may work twenty hours a day—corporate America loves this one—seek to save the world through medicine, go to the moon, obsess about professional sports, or become overinvolved with kids, friends, or church. Again, we addict to anything that keeps us *preoccupied* and *unavailable* to our spouse and kids, where we perceive our greatest emotional threat. So our families feel neglected and ignored, and their reactive defenses come up, and ours come out even higher, and we all wind up in a terrible chaotic mess.

And of course millions of us addict through chemistry—alcohol and other drugs. These particular addictions present additional danger to our families and the rest of society, because alcohol and other drugs ultimately make us *crazy*. These chemicals replace the normal chemistry of the brain, so that those who use them actually cannot think straight. Ultimately, addicts lose their minds by keeping their brain chemistry confused and unable to function as it is designed. And they make their families feel crazy as well. Anyone who's lived with an alcoholic or a drug addict *feels crazy* much of the time, and gets mired in the chaos created by the addict and his or her chemicals. Family members feel a constant anger and anxiety about the addict's determination to self-destruct.

Self-medication doesn't help. When a person addicts by means of a chemical—say the natural depressant alcohol, or a "street" chemical, or prescription chemicals—he or she is ingesting a substance that will alter the actual brain chemistry. The result is manipulation of the mood and emotions—ups and downs, highs and lows of the person.

Why would we want something to alter our mood or manipulate our emotions? I believe we do it because it gives the impression of quick relief for feelings of depression or anxiety about our lives. Many times alcoholics and addicts are self-medicating their feelings, even though consciously they aren't even aware of their true feelings.

Time and again when I confront chemical addicts with the question, "Would you be willing to take proper medication under a physician's care for your anxiety or depression?" the sincere response comes back: "No, I won't take medication, because I'm not depressed or anxious, and I don't like to take pills or put foreign stuff in my body." And these are educated, professional people speaking!

That's one small example of the colossal power of denial that blossoms inside the addict's brain.

Using alcohol and other drugs to deal with emotions is like a two-edged sword. On one hand, they can provide nearly instant relief. The brain chemistry is altered quickly, so the relief comes instantly. There's no need to wait and sit with the misery until the problem gets worked out. The pain goes away, fast.

Certainly our society would have us believe that's what the good life is all about—avoid discomfort, feel good all the time.

Then, too, many of us watched our own parents deal with the discomforts of life by drinking, drugging, being sick and taking prescription drugs, binge eating, throwing up, not eating, working excessively, being depressed, and drowning in depression, anxiety, or both. No one imagines that's a picture of having a good life, and none of us would wish a life of chemical dependency or any other addiction on our kids or anyone we love. Yet escaping and avoiding relationships—especially conflicts—by using our addictions is exactly what we are modeling for the young people in our lives and the next generation.

Until we learn healthier ways of doing relationships, we will do anything and everything except work through conflict and resolve our differences in ways that are healthy for both partners.

The powerful denial system. Addictive behavior varies little from one person to another, except perhaps in degree. All addicts exhibit similar traits, and they seem surprised to know that their behaviors are *right out of the textbook*. All addictions progress along a predictable path. The first and foremost trait of any addict is to *deny* that whatever he's doing could be considered an addiction. In my entire professional career, I cannot remember ever confronting a person about being an addict and have that person agree, regardless of the evidence. The usual response is, "Oh, I can quit whenever I want to." It's been said addiction is the only disease that insists you don't have it.

No one ever sets out intentionally to become an addict, and since addictions gain their power slowly and non-forcefully, we—the addict and the family both—fail to realize what is happening. Even when the behavior has moved from "just a pleasurable experience" to an addiction, the addiction has already robbed us of our awareness about it. Denial has set in, and the addiction has taken control of both the addict's and the family's life.

Our denial systems are able to accommodate enormous amounts of evidence without our linking any of it to having an addiction. Because we have such a broad range of addictions and addictive behaviors, the general public identifies only a tiny 5% core of our addictive population as addicts. That 5% core will indeed exhibit strong evidence of addiction—for example, a skid-row bum passed out in the gutter. "Yes, of course that's an addict!" people quickly say. "Anybody can see that."

But what about the other 95% of white- and blue-collar workers who are also addicts but, unlike the bum, haven't yet lost it all? Helping professionals may describe such persons as "functional addicts" or "functional alcoholics." They go to work every day, support their families, pay their taxes, don't get locked up. Yet they use their addictions as a way of escaping the realities of daily life, until circumstances force them to face the truth of their life, or lose it.

It's both amazing and sad how few addicts see any connection between their use of chemicals, sex, food, money, etc., and their lack of a productive, satisfying life and their string of broken relationships, including marriages and kids. Whenever you go over the addict's laundry list of broken relationships, lost jobs, so-called bad luck, and health and money problems, the addict will attribute every difficulty in his or her life to anything and everything other than those addictions.

Three identifying traits. Three specific defenses of addicts keep their denial systems intact:

1. *Blame.* According to the addict, the problems the addiction creates are everyone's fault except his own;
2. *Unwillingness to be accountable or responsible* for the consequences the addictive behaviors create; and
3. *Control.* Addicts feel controlled by everyone and everything in life. Their generalized feeling of victimization keeps the *blame cycle* going.

Addictions require us to use all these maneuvers, because if we stop blaming and actually look honestly at the consequences we're creating, we will have to move out of our denial, and in order to continue avoiding reality and practicing the addiction, we must maintain that denial. We cling fast to these addictive defenses, because if we ever let them go, we will have to grow up, move out of the Victim Box, and start taking adult responsibility for our life.

Abandoning relationships, even though there's a better way. Countless numbers of high-performing, high-level corporate professionals make the decision to give up their families and "move on to better things" while living their lives under the influence of alcohol, other drugs, or both. They do this because they have never learned the necessary skills for *staying with their emotional discomfort* long enough to learn what it's about and work through it to a healthy resolution—a task no one can accomplish while under the influence of mind-altering chemicals.

Likewise, countless Americans in the middle and lower socioeconomic classes make the same foolish decision to give up on their relationships, because chemicals prevent them from thinking clearly enough and long enough to stay with their discomfort and work things out with their spouses and kids. Tragically, probably none of these people would ever have made that decision without the brain-dulling assistance of chemicals.

Two flavors of defense. Addicts use behavioral defenses to keep their addictions going, and those defenses come in just two flavors: being *aggressive* or being *pitiful*. All their defenses will fall into these two categories, and others who have to deal with them—family members in particular—will tend to be angry, anxious, or feel sorry for them most of the time.

When addicts are acting with *aggression*, they behave like the bully on the playground, using intimidation to get their way.

When addicts are acting *pitiful* they are often crying, sick, need help, can't help themselves, isolating, talking about wanting to die, maybe even threatening to die.

Both these defenses constitute a tactic called *emotional blackmail*. Emotional blackmail sends the message, "I will scare you enough so that you'll give me life the way I want it," or "I will scare you enough that you'll get out of my way, stop confronting me, stop naming me an addict, and stop saying I'm addicting, so I can keep doing my addicting in peace."

Other identifying traits serve to keep addicts in denial as well. One is *a notable lack of empathy and connection with others,* especially family. Addicts tend to isolate from their families, if not physically, at least emotionally, because addicts know that those who genuinely love them are probably going to confront their craziness at some point

Then, too, addicts are often *grandiose and arrogant, with an inflated sense of entitlement.* They view themselves *above* all the mess they are told they are creating and declare everyone else "crazy."

Self-pity is in the picture as well. An addicted person usually feels sorry for himself or herself, feeling constantly deprived. In fact, all addicts *believe themselves to be victims* and act like it, seemingly controlled by everyone and everything in their lives. They tell anyone who will listen about all the injustices they've had to endure in their lives.

Magical thinking is another defense that keeps the addict believing the rules apply— only to everyone else. The addict thinks he can drive and drink and no one will get hurt, or that she doesn't have to stay in recovery, go to Twelve-Step groups, or— heaven forbid—have to actually *work* the Twelve Steps, because she can handle her addictions.

Addicts are *critical of any form of authority*—parents, spouse, boss, government, law enforcement, school systems, churches. Living as if *at the mercy of* everybody and everything, they resist authority, responsibility, accountability, and place themselves above all people or systems that could stand in the way of them doing what they want, which is to use their addictions to escape their misery.

Meanness and paranoia surface with many addicts. They often believe everyone else is out to get them, and they become aggressive and vindictive as a way to protect their perceived right to stay addicted and thereby destroy their lives and the lives of those who care about them.

Unrecovered addicts *lack the ability to be humble*, which keeps them unteachable. They're quick to let anyone know that they don't need help. To the addict's way of thinking, you're the one who is wrong, out of line, and you better mind your own business!

Addicts are *blind to how the consequences of their choices of behaviors affect others*, especially those who love them. They really believe they can go on addicting, and things will work out for everyone.

The list of defenses is elaborate and seemingly endless. They *romanticize* their addictions, glorify any positive features to their addictions, and fail to look at the harmful effects. They only see the happy/fun/escape part of their addictive lives.

They *mystify their addictive process*, using the reasoning that "Something just came over me," or "It just happened," or "The Devil made me do it." Such thinking blocks their awareness that they themselves are *choosing* to do these things, so that they find it more comfortable to believe some outside force is determining their behavior—the victim role again.

Often addicts describe others who have overcome addictions or never used them as "stronger" than they, when in fact it's the addict who *is not choosing to use his or her own strengths*. People who *appear* stronger are simply people who are *choosing to use their strengths*.

Terminal uniqueness is the comprehensive, fatal "out" for all addicts. Every addict believes his own addictions and addictive processes are unique. He may say, "You just don't understand because you don't want to, or because you aren't hooked into smoking (drinking, drugging, using sex, money, gambling, or whatever)." When first introduced to Twelve-Step programs, addicts often say, "It's all right for them, but I'm not like those people. *My case is different*. I don't belong here." The really sad part about the fallacy of *terminal uniqueness* is that many addicts die of their addictions still believing themselves and their situation unique, while in our society today addictions are actually more common than dirt.

Addicts *use vagueness to avoid awareness*, because awareness points to choices and responsibility. Addicts often answer "I don't know," or "I don't remember," when someone asks them to be accountable. They don't want to see choices. They believe they don't have choices, that life is "being done" to them.

An addict *perceives control as coming from everyone else, including the entire universe*, when it is actually coming from the addiction. The addiction is what gains total control of the addict's life and makes him or her believe the addiction is essential for survival. That is the most powerful control the addict experiences. Those people who love and care most about the addict, however, who are trying to get the addict to stop the self-destructive behavior, are seen by the addict as the most controlling of all. Thus the addict's concerned and caring family and friends become, in his or her eyes, the enemy.

Addicts live the life of paupers—not necessarily in the economic sense, but in the emotional sense. All human beings desire connection to others, but addicts remove themselves from that possibility. As victims to their addictions, even if they have plenty of money, they lack the ability to stay connected to those persons who love and care about them the most.

Addicts are children in grown-up bodies who never felt parented and usually felt deprived of enough parental love. Many of them remain stuck in this childlike place for the rest of their lives. Although they are very lonely, empty people, they will fight to keep people away from them who will notice their addictions, confront them, and offer to help them go into treatment or other recovery work.

Because their family and close friends are the only people who genuinely love them, by distancing from those people, they deprive themselves of the very love they need and want the most.

Addicts require Enablers/Rescuers. Addicts must be in relationships with people who will addict with them, or else (and they usually prefer this) just sleepwalk through the relationship, never noticing, never confronting, never speaking of—The Problem—someone who can easily be shut up by intimidation or pity.

Partners of addicts are sometimes called *enablers,* because their behaviors make it possible for the addict to continue addicting by covering up for them, waking them up, lying for them, rationalizing their inappropriateness, excusing them, forgiving them, trying harder to please them, running interference for them with the family, friends, and work problems, and cooking, cleaning, and doing enough for them in hopes that the addict will quit their addictions.

Another word for *enabler* is *rescuer.* The rescuer "drives an ambulance" through life, rescuing those who refuse to be responsible for their behaviors. Rescuers are constantly alert to crises, ready at a moment's notice to save the day. Rescuers thrive on preventing a crisis, never realizing that *a crisis may need to happen to wake the addict up.* On the other hand, rescuers have been known to *create* a crisis if one hasn't happened in a while, giving them an opportunity for a big rescue-effort moment, especially if the addict seems appreciative and grateful for their help. Rescuers pride themselves on being good mind-readers. They can figure out what everyone wants without ever being told, and they frequently offer help before they're ever asked.

What enablers and rescuers are blind to is that their rescuing and enabling behaviors are the main reason the addict can continue addicting. I have seen cases where a hardened addict quits addicting completely when the chief enabler or rescuer is lost and does not fall back into the addictions unless either the old enabler returns to take up the rescuing behavior again, or else the addict comes up with a new rescuer. This is not necessarily conscious behavior on the part of the addict. Yet all addicts know at some level that they need at least one rescuer willing to pay the consequences of the addiction, so that he or she can continue addicting.

Enablers and rescuers are as addicted to the addict and all that comes packaged with the addict's life as the addict is to his drugs of choice. They may become indignant if such a thing is suggested, but the fact is that they have shaped their own lives around the life of their addicts. Enablers live by the addict's rules and never question or ask for explanations, never expect participation from a partner—no team effort—and, most importantly, tolerate totally inappropriate behaviors. Above all, they *never* use the forbidden words "alcoholic," "drug addict," "gambler," "workaholic," "sexaholic," "shopaholic," or any other word that implies an addiction. They walk all around The Problem but never name it.

Enablers are able to live by a lot of these unspoken rules because they are the products of parents who were addicts or depressed, pitiful (didn't take care of themselves physically, emotionally, spiritually) or angry, sick, or powerless. Some of their families of origin were so fearful of conflict that they dismissed, minimized, or avoided discussion of anything unpleasant, to the point that life and the world were never dealt with in a realistic way. Enablers who came from such families are unrealistic, too trusting of others, and have never learned to trust their own inner instincts or knowledge. And when you remember that millions of Americans come from such families, you see the problem doesn't affect only a few people, it affects millions of us as well.

Rescuers tend to sleepwalk through life, caretaking, accommodating, and doing everything possible to keep life on an even keel, regardless of what is really happening. Enablers can easily be bullied, intimidated, shamed, teased, emotionally blackmailed, and guilted, from speaking up to their addict. *Enablers and rescuers manage to avoid their own pain by focusing on the addict.* Addictive behavior is so disruptive to life that running damage control for the addict becomes a full-time job, leaving the enabler no time or energy to focus on whatever pain may be there deep down inside himself or herself.

Rescuers find it very difficult if not impossible to allow the addict or anyone else to *sit in the discomfort of their pain*. They cannot allow the addict to experience the consequences of his or her addictive choices, believing that it will "upset" or even "destroy" the addict, when in fact, having the addict to experience the consequences of their behaviors is often the first step in saving addicts' lives.

As long as the enabler will follow the addict's rules—doesn't make waves, keeps life as smooth as possible in spite of the chaos—life with the addict can go on forever. The addict's greatest *risk*, perhaps the only one, is that one day the enabler or rescuer may wake up. If or when that day comes, everything will change.

The role of conflict. Recent research tells us that in this country *the number-one predictor of divorce is the habitual avoidance of conflict.* With half of all marriages ending in divorce, we may safely assume that huge numbers of Americans are habitually sidestepping or stalling around any conflict in their marriages. The conflict is there, all right; they just ignore it, pretend it doesn't exist—in other words, they're sleepwalking.

And I believe that our number-one method for avoiding conflict is—you guessed it—falling back on addictions. When we addict, we become masters at *justifying* whatever we are doing. The addict or alcoholic can always be counted on to come up with myriad reasons why he must behave the way he does, and every excuse makes perfect sense to him, even when the behavior is destroying the marriage. In fact, the marriage itself often gets the blame: "No wonder I drink. Anybody would, married to a nag (or gambler, or womanizer, or workaholic) like you!"

If couples stuck in this hellish life do try to resolve conflict with the only methods they know, one partner decides to give in, then later resents having done so, or else forces the other partner to give in, which that partner also comes to resent.

Who is teaching conflict resolution? We wonder why our kids are fighting each other, bullying, hating and looking for revenge, even carrying guns to school. Could it be because they don't see us resolving our conflicts with our partners or with them, they follow our lead and fall back on the easy way out? They may do drugs, have sex, get a gun, or blame the school, police, society and any other authority that might require them to be accountable for their choices of behavior. The old adage has it right. *Our children usually don't do as we say, they do as we do.* Not every out-of-control child has out-of-control parents, but parents' inability to work through differences in healthy ways is often mirrored in children who have no model or way to learn these vital skills.

The role of feelings. Dealing in a healthy, realistic way with feelings is one of the most difficult tasks facing the addict. Many addicts seized their earliest opportunity to avoid experiencing their true feelings, substituting numbed-out, drugged ones to ease their emotional pain. As strange as it may sound, there are people who started drinking and drugging as teenagers who haven't experienced an authentic feeling since that time. One response to experiencing authentic feelings for the first time may take the form of *panic attacks.* Addicts have learned no coping skills for real feelings, accustomed only to the fake, dead-like ones chemicals produce.

They have to start from scratch learning how to deal with life on an authentic basis. It's as if they are waking up from a deep, anesthetized sleep and have no awareness of life with real feelings and without chemicals. The earlier in life a person began resorting to chemicals for relief, the harder these life skills will be to learn. To experience an authentic feeling is devastating to these people. The normal levels of anxiety nonaddicted human beings feel is absolutely overwhelming for people who never learned what to do with their feelings other than kill them, especially the three big: SAD, MAD, and AFRAID.

Learning to sit with our pain. When we're addicting, covering up our emotions, acting like they aren't really there, disconnected from our true feelings, we are in no state to have healthy relationships. And until we learn the importance of doing it and how to do it, none of us wants to sit with our psychic pain, so we usually react with some immediate action designed to help us escape the pain or the thought of it. We learned to do this as children, because we had very few if any people who wanted to help us with emotional pain or even knew how. When others saw us uncomfortable with any emotion, their first instinct was to help us get away from it: "Here, have a cookie!" or "Just get over it!" or "C'mon, let's do something fun!" or "Crybaby!" or "I'm gonna tell!" and a hundred similar avoidance tactics.

Consequently, what we learned about having unpleasant feelings was that we shouldn't be having them. "Something must be wrong with me!" As we grew up with this deeply ingrained notion about emotional discomfort, we began to care for ourselves according to the same dogma that our caregivers used: *Avoid unpleasant feelings like the plague! Instead,, hurry up and do something that feels good! There's something very wrong with a person who has unpleasant emotions and feelings.*

Bad news and good news. Living with addicted people isn't pleasant. I know that fact well, having grown up with two chemically addicted parents. I watched two intelligent, gifted, worthwhile people waste their own lives and devastate their children. *If you're a parent who seeks relief from life stresses by drinking or using mind-altering drugs, please abandon right now the belief that it doesn't affect your kids.* It *does* affect them, in ways that will hamper them throughout life unless the entire family gets some education and help around the issue of addictions. That's the bad news.

The *good* news is that there is plenty each of us can do about the situation, once we reach adulthood. Times are changing, fortunately, and when a person of any age—teens to seniors—chooses the avoidance path that addictions provide, rather than taking responsibility for behaviors and consequences, families no longer have to endure decades or even lifetimes of rescuing or picking up the pieces. The addictive behavior can be addressed, and effective steps to remedy matters can follow.

As an adult, time and again I have seen the empowerment knowledge brings, the effectiveness of learning skills and gaining tools to solve problems and work through conflict, instead of staying defeated and imprisoned by painful emotions. Much of my professional life centers on supporting individuals or family members who have made the decision to live life differently, learn how to handle emotions in a healthy way, and build fulfilling relationships. It is well worth the effort!

Chapter 10

Stepping out of the Victim Box

"But it's not my fault!"

Life in the Victim Box is a dog's life. Those of us who inhabit the Victim Box never learned to take care of ourselves emotionally. The Victim Box is a mindset that keeps us stuck in that helpless, powerless place we were in as children, living at the mercy of circumstance and choices made by other people—the adults in our lives, sometimes older siblings and other children, including bullies. The victim in all of us is that part of us that did not have our emotional needs met in good enough ways when we were children.

We had no significant power or control over our lives, because the adults had it all. That's the natural order of life. The job of parents is to love, nurture, and keep kids safe enough while they learn about life and develop into independent, capable, and reliable people. Children's lives are literally in the hands of their caregivers .

If the caregivers are nurturing and caring, those kids are fortunate. If they're cold and cruel, then those kids find it harder to survive. If they are sometimes cold and sometimes caring, those kids get confused—torn between feeling cared for and having to fend for themselves.

No matter which fate was ours, in the ideal circumstance, we would reach adulthood knowing it's time to move out of that powerlessness, take charge of our lives, and set healthy personal limits and boundaries. Did it happen like that? Probably not.

Boundaries matter. Most of us did not learn how to do these things because *our parents didn't know how to set their own healthy personal boundaries.* More often than not, they were all over any boundaries we tried to have, all over our personal space, and all over each other's boundaries and personal space as well. The result was that we never saw healthy boundaries modeled, nor had anybody teach us two crucial concepts:

1) Personal boundaries exist with healthy individuals, and
2) All of us need to have, set, and hold them for ourselves if we ever intend to have connected, healthy, loving relationships (see Chapter 7).

As children, if we stood up for ourselves to some adult, we were usually considered sassy or disrespectful. And being sassy or disrespectful brought unpleasant punishment. So, being resourceful and wanting to survive, we learned to compensate for the fact that other people held the power over our lives.

Compensating with defenses. Many of us learned to *cooperate*, even when the adult with the power was being unreasonable; to *rationalize* the behavior of the adults; *minimize* our own needs; or *go outside the accepted system* to get our needs met when adults' misuse of their power over us left us feeling vulnerable. In order to feel powerful, some of us learned to *bully and intimidate*, copying the behavior of the adults in our lives. Bullies are made, not born. Although these methods worked for us as kids, they don't serve us well as adults if we seek to have connected relationships and emotional health.

What we needed to be taught. Our parents could have helped us learn more of what we needed in those formative years by encouraging us to

1)   talk about how we were feeling,
2)   tell truthfully how our lives were going,
3)   ask for what we were needing,
4)   have those needs met, at least some of the time, and, most critically,
5)   learn how to resolve conflict instead of avoiding it.

And through all of that we needed parents to model these healthy behaviors and listen to us without reacting by judging, accusing, or blaming.

The avoidance strategies we learned—denying, hiding, minimizing, distracting, attacking, and bullying—were the ways the adults in our lives operated as we watched and modeled our behaviors on theirs. *Each one of these avoidance maneuvers is a victim defense.* Never mind that when we have a bully in our face, the bully seems powerful, not weak. Someone who resorts to bullying, along with any other avoidance method, is still trapped in the Victim Box.

The Victim life. Any time we avoid the real problem instead of addressing it, we miss the opportunity to work toward mutual resolution of the problem and stay connected. Chances are, we heard our parents complain and criticize each other, like pitiful victims, instead of being able to watch them resolve their conflicts and teach us to do the same. What did we learn? To complain, criticize, and stay in the Victim Box ourselves.

The person in the Victim Box never taps into her or his own personal power. She believes that doing so would upset a lot of people, and a true Victim knows the price of upsetting people, especially those she loves. She lives in the past or the future, just as she did as a child, afraid to express her true feelings unless she can be sure of pleasant results. He learned to deny his own reality and hope that avoiding "trouble" will bring him love.

Victim language. Victims use the language of a child: "I *can't* do (this or that)," or "I *can't* afford to buy that," or "I *can't* take any more!"

Adult language says, "*I've made a conscious decision* not to take any more," or "*I've made a choice* to not buy that." In working with adults who use this Victim style of language, I point out that just the word "*can't*" automatically places them at the mercy of something or someone.

You will not hear a Victim say, "*I put myself* into a position in my relationships that ended up hurtful to me." The Victim says, "*I was put . . .*" or "*I allowed myself to be put* into a position that . . .*"

Victims feel totally controlled by others, and either become helplessly compliant, so that they never say "No" to anyone, or so defiantly oppositional that they refuse to even take a suggestion.

Victim disguises. Victims wear masks of various types to hide their fears, ranging from the grandiose bully and tyrant to the pitiful weeper and complainer. Victims can appear in many disguises. Whichever one he or she chooses, however, a time bomb is ticking as the Victim goes through each day, trying to keep the peace (the Pleaser), intimidating others (the Bully or Rager), not mentioning her own wants and needs (the Martyr), being pitiful and helpless (the Powerless One), being blamed (the Scapegoat), or helping anyone and everyone else, to her own detriment (the Rescuer).

The time bomb is ticking, all right, and the length of the countdown depends upon how long this scenario goes on before the Victim realizes his or her behavior won't change a thing. Regardless of whether the Victim makes great sacrifices—while failing to speak up about his or her own reality—those expectations he harbors for a satisfactory outcome are never met, so that resentments continue to build. Eventually, the Victim will blow up, threaten, run away, or lash out (most common in male Victims, who disguise fear as anger), or (more often for female Victims) get physically sick, perhaps purging herself of everything she's been stuffing inside, or at least maneuvering herself into some situation—a hospital, for example—where she can feel cared for by others .

When we give up our power. Most of us learned another lesson from childhood as well: "Never, never, *never* come out and directly ask for what you want and need emotionally in a relationship, because that is selfish and egotistical and sinful!" But what happens if we don't directly ask for what we want and need in a relationship? The people we're trying to be in relationship with must try to read our minds, which is impossible, so that we wind up living at the mercy of what *they think* we want and need. As Victims, too busy taking care of others, while sacrificing our wants and needs to theirs, we abandon the responsibility of caring for ourselves, leaving everyone else to do it for us. We've relinquished the power to manage our own lives, turning over that responsibility to others. Victims are not proactive on their own behalf. They stand back and wait for others to create a space for them, hoping others will make room for their personal reality in relationships.

But here's what actually happens. Those to whom the Victim gives up power do *not* take care of the Victim as he or she needs or wants. And when those others leave the Victim to do the work of making his or her own way in the relationship and the world, Victims get pitiful or indignant. They fear rejection so greatly that they won't even try to be responsible for themselves, leaving it to others to take care of them, even though the others make it apparent they don't intend to do it.

So, while Victims may appear to be weak and powerless, *they are actually running the show* by making sure everybody else is taking care of them, or trying to make everybody else feel guilty if all their needs and wants aren't met. It's a Catch-22, because they *refuse to let others know their true feelings, their wants and needs, or their true reality*, so obviously no one else can figure out those needs or meet them, even if they wanted to do so.

The Victim arranges matters to guarantee failure of the relationship. The adult Victim is still the Victim child, who never knew it was okay and healthy to speak up about such personal matters as feelings with anyone. Because Victims refuse to take the risk of speaking up on their own behalf, they often pout, sulk, sigh, or complain. Or they may become resentful, threatening, pitiful, sick, withdrawn, depressed, anxious, and left out of life. The fear of rejection and abandonment is very fresh in their minds, playing a dominant part in all their relationships. They fail to recognize that nobody enjoys being in relationship with someone who's pouting, sulking, complaining, resentful, sighing, pitiful, sick, withdrawn, depressed, anxious, or sitting on life's sidelines. So when others turn away from them, they get the very thing they most fear—rejection and abandonment.

Victims can grow, thank goodness. The growth challenge for Victims is to learn how to share their wants and needs with those they love, and to expect their loved ones to share the same with them. How sad that most of us grew up with such embedded lessons on holding back our feelings and realities from each other at this intimate level. *True intimacy between two persons is not possible unless they do learn to share in this way.* Authentic sharing and true intimacy are two of life's most powerful bonding tools.

As children, we not only learned it was "wrong" to talk about our personal wants and needs, but we saw our parents refusing to do so as well. Children learn what they see, and no one modeled this skill for us. What we did see our grown-up family members modeling was the opposite—being Victims themselves.

You can see then, that being a Victim is a learned behavior, and can therefore be unlearned. Isn't that great news? Remaining closed down emotionally is not natural—think of the baby who lets you know at every minute whether things are going pleasantly or unpleasantly in its little life. But later on, as we grow, we begin to perceive that sometimes the price of letting it all out is too high, so we learn to keep ourselves shut down, first emotionally, then in every way.

Getting out of the box. A great paradox about victimhood is that the Victim seldom realizes what an terribly narrow and limited view of life he or she has had, or what an extremely limited life she or he has lived until some crisis comes, and education or counseling unlatches the door of the box to let in the bright light of day. We all deserve hopes and dreams, yet realizing those hopes and dreams is impossible so long as we give them all over into other people's keeping.

The choice is always an individual one. One last point to ponder about sharing our wants and needs with our partners and family: just because we learn to voice our personal wants and needs does not mean we will or even should get what we ask. Speaking up is about taking care of ourselves. The others to whom we express our wants and needs on this genuine level have a choice of how to respond—help us get some of our needs met, or refuse. They can choose to share with us in return, or stay distant and defended in their own Victim Box.

Learning this skill—asking for what we want and need—and using it means only that we are making every effort to take care of ourselves emotionally, by voicing these desires instead of *acting them out* onto others. At least if we speak them, we open the possibility to talk about them and the opportunity to come to some resolution around them. Hiding this information from ourselves and others is what makes us escape into our own addictions and avoid each other.

The alternative to learning this new way. Unfortunately, in many segments of our society, addictions—alcohol, other drugs, workaholism, affairs, money, religiosity—are seen as a more acceptable method of coping with life. Heaven forbid that someone should talk about their worries and stresses, or get these things *said out loud* to each other and begin seeking resolution to their problems! Because we never learned and were never allowed to do that as children, far too many of us go on believing it's taboo to *say out loud to our partner* what is really bothering us. Isn't that ridiculous? Of course it is, but most of us still live like that.

Until they've been shown a better way, many in our society continue to believe it's better to keep quiet and not "hurt someone's feelings" than to speak up with their truth, and even worse, that it's better to divorce than to say things that might upset your partner! It takes courage to do it differently, to take the risk of being vulnerable so that we can connect in a healthy way with our partner and our kids. Only when we choose to be honest about identifying our needs, open up, and express them appropriately, and step out of the protection of the Victim Box will we move into a healthy life with connected relationships.

Harville Hendrix and Helen Hunt make a strong point about how we human beings can intervene upon our own behaviors, consciously stop our hurtful reactivity, and replace it with healthier, higher-functioning interactions. This is wonderful news, because it says we are not *at the mercy of anyone or anything*—not our feelings, thoughts, reality, unconscious mind, or our *natural instincts*. If we have someone in our life who cares for us enough to tell us, gently and kindly, about our defensive behaviors, we can use that person's input and actually intervene upon ourselves to change those behaviors into positive energy.

Here is a tried-and-true exercise to do with your partner, so that both of you can begin the experience of hearing each other's reality and ask for what you want and need in the relationship without judgment or reactivity. Be sure to use the Intentional Dialogue Process throughout this exercise (see Chapter 4 for the format). The boldface sections are what the dissatisfied partner says:

1. **When you** _____(be specific in describing partner's behavior), as

"When you agreed to go over the bills with me last Saturday and didn't, and also didn't even mention that topic with me or say you'd changed your mind,"
Receiver mirrors and validates and says, "Tell me more."

2. **I feel** _____(use one of more feeling words), as "discounted, ignored, betrayed, suspicious,"etc.
   Receiver mirrors and validates and says, "Tell me more."

3. **And I conclude from your behavior or words that**_____
   (whatever meaning you assign to their behavior/words, you make up from your own history), as "I conclude you don't care about me or what's important to me, that you believe you can ignore me and not live up to our agreements or even let me know you've changed your mind. I conclude I don't matter to you."
   Receiver mirrors, validates, expresses empathy, and says, "Tell me more."

4. **What I need from you now is** _____(give partner a do-able behavior or something specific to say on a regular basis that would feel less hurtful than the present approach to the issue), as: "I want you to set a time and place for us to go over the bills together, and if you change your mind or won't be at that time and place, tell me at least 24 hours before and reset a time and place to meet and go over the bills."
   Receiver mirrors, validates, and agrees to what partner is asking or can ask for two more ideas. If he or she is willing to try a new way of operating in this relationship, Receiver will choose and commit to meeting at least one of those requests.

Accepting the opportunity of this format requires both partners to stretch and grow. Of course, Receiver will have some issue also around this problem of going over the bills, since both partners are affected by any issue that arises in their marriage. One partner holds one point of view and one holds the other side. The Receiver can then use this same format to have his or her side aired and dealt with respectfully, after the couple has taken a sufficient break from this subject—usually six hours at least.

Chapter 11

Getting Real

"Are we ready to tell it like it is?"

Learning to live in the present moment means developing an awareness high enough to cut through our defenses and say what's really going on with us, instead of struggling to defend ourselves against whatever is happening. Being real means to become willing to speak our feelings to another person and accept the results. It also means looking honestly at our own words and actions to see what part they have played in perpetuating a problem.

If my relationship with my partner isn't going as I would like, I must first ask myself what I'm doing or saying to avoid telling my partner how I really feel:

Am I withdrawing from or avoiding my partner?
Am I tired, depressed, anxious, busy, angry, or disappointed?
Do I yell?
Maybe I opt out: "Relationships are so hard, I just don't have the energy to work on ours."
Or maybe I'm sighing, or sarcastic, or critical.
Do I get sick and become automatically unavailable?

All the behaviors mentioned above are defenses against saying what is actually going on with me right now in the relationship. My defenses are things I use to keep from being real.

And when we don't speak up, making such feeling statements as "I feel discounted," or "I feel scared of being abandoned," or "I feel unimportant," "I feel lonely," or "Maybe I fear you value other people or things more than me," we are keeping secrets from our partner.

Poisoning the relationship. So long as we keep secrets in an effort to protect ourselves from discomfort in a relationship, we invite *toxicity* into that relationship. We fail to see that by keeping secrets, we kill the *alive* energy in the relationship—the part of the relationship that feels the best, the part that makes us the happiest and most content.

Let's be clear on what constitutes secrets in relationships. *A secret is anything I'm not telling you because of some unspoken agenda on my part.* Here are some examples of how and why we keep secrets and what can happen when we do.

1) *I hold back from telling you something about my reality— my feelings—because "I don't want to hurt your feelings."*

Suppose I'm angry with you about something you said or did that wounded me. But because I don't want to hurt *your* feelings, instead of telling you straightforwardly how I feel about what happened, I clam up and say nothing. And if I'm really honest with myself, I have to admit I'm not being straight with you because of how I think you will react when you "get your feelings hurt." I fear you will attack me or disapprove of me.

Once I do that—hold back my truth—things between us change. Now my energy is different with you. you—the other person—can feel the difference, although you may not consciously understand what is happening between us. And so you draw back too, and now your energy will also be different with me. As we both protect our vulnerabilities from each other, both of us lose the connection we had in our relationship.

2) *Or maybe I disagree with you about something—raising kids, money, your parents, sex, religion—but when I try to talk to you about the topic, you react in a way that feels threatening to me.*

You get angry, or promise to do things differently but never do or shut down ignore me, reject me, cry, yell, or do things that I feel helpless against. And having had that unpleasant experience, I quit telling you my truth. So whatever issues is the basis of the problem gets shoved under the rug and smolders there until it bursts into flame again. I remain guarded and miss out on the satisfying completeness, the freedom of sharing everything with you in our relationship.

3) *I begin to hide what I am doing to soothe my wounded soul.*

Pay particular attention to this one, because keeping secrets is a necessary dynamic in addictive behavior. May I drink, drug, (including smoke, dip, chew, snort, shoot sup), have affairs, gamble, spend money, work or stay busy, get obsessed with any project, get over-involved with the kids—do anything, in fact, except talk to you about my misery. You then pull away to seek *alive* energy in some different person or place, because it's no longer available with me.

4) *I change the subject and manipulate and maneuver around the facts. I tell you what I think you want to hear, in the way I think will cause the least trouble, and no more.*

5) *I "forget" or "fail to remember" something as it's presented to me, learning to disassociate or have spells of lost memory to protect myself from painful realities.*

I wind up with a doctored version of life, that works against me and the relationship.

6) *I get aggressive and accuse others rather than look at myself.*

When a subject I don't want addressed comes up, I intimidate, bully, or blame my partner, for fear of having my secrets exposed, until he or she shuts up. As a result my partner pulls away from me or resents me, may feel cowed and unworthy, may even begin to doubt their own grasp on reality.

7) *I do anything and everything to avoid having my truth exposed, except just telling my partner that I feel threatened, scared, lonely, worried about losing our marriage, disappointed, betrayed, whatever my truth is.*

Yet, as I withhold my truth from the relationship, I disrespect my partner by not trusting him or her to know and accept me as I really am.

Leaving childhood to become partners. These are all learned behaviors, learned when we were children. They are behaviors we took on so survive because most of us were afraid to tell our parents our truth. Now, as adults, we transfer that same fear of rejection and ultimate abandonment onto our partners, and we withhold our truth from them as well. But it doesn't have to stay that way. Partners are not our parents.

By not speaking up and saying our truth, we are keeping secrets, and secrets drain the aliveness out of relationships. Then, once the aliveness is drained away, we don't want the relationship any more. It feels dead It no longer feels good

Think of what happens if you were to eat all the icing off your birthday cake, before you ate any cake. With no icing, if you're like most people, you wouldn't like the cake any more, you'd just want to throw it away. That's exactly what happens when we let the vitality leak out of our relationships. And yes, I did say "let." *This is a choice.*

Getting real takes two. We can either accept a relationship that's not fulfilling and suffer along in it, knowing it won't get any better, or we can do something about our own behavior to get "more real" and ask our partner to help us in this endeavor. We actually need that partner's input in order to get real, since we can only experience life as it appears to us *from behind our own* *eyes.* Learning to partner requires someone who will work with us, supplying us with valuable information about how they experience us so we can begin to alter our hurtful behaviors according to their input. We must also be willing to be equally real with our partners about their behavior and help them learn new, less damaging ways to interact with us.

Two-way conversations. Sometimes partners only want to give input, not receive it. If that's the case, I encourage the partner who wants a more real relationship to use the input given by the partner anyway, make changes in his or her own behavior, and stay focused on his or her own efforts. As one partner changes and gets healthier in relationships, the less dysfunction that partner will tolerate in any relationship, so changes will come regardless of whether both partners are actively involved.

Getting real means that we choose to step out of that dark place we've been living in to let our partner see us as we really are, in order to grow past those limited childlike reactions we adopted when we felt threatened. We invite our partner to do the same and become willing to work through any problems that arise from all this truthfulness and openness. Sure, it's scary, but it's the only way to have a relationship that's *real,* rather than one that's just going through some motions and creating a nice picture.

But how do we do this, getting real? What does *being real* require of us? First, it demands that we say honestly what's going on with us right now, regardless of whether it might "hurt somebody's feelings," "make somebody mad," or "cause problems."

Of course this doesn't mean we should say things like, "You're the biggest bully in the world and I hate you." That's an *attack,* and it only makes the relationship worse. If I feel like saying something so attacking, it would benefit me more to peel away that layer of anger in myself and see what vulnerable place it's covering. And in every case, I will find that my *anger is always covering up pain of some sort.*

Destructive methods of communication destroy relationships, because they *break the connection.* We can learn to express our reality in ways that are *real and genuine,* without attacking the other person or putting him or her on the defensive. One of the most productive ways we can handle this kind of anger is to pause and discover what pain we are hiding and address that pain instead of the anger that is hiding it. Then we share this information with our partners and suggest:

1) what they could do to help us get some of our needs met around this pain,

2) ways they could alter their hurtful behaviors.

Starting before it's too late. In marriages, if couples were able to say to each other—and the earlier in the marriage the better—"I'm not happy in our marriage and I don't know why," they could get busy identifying what's going on, resolving their differences, and using most of their energy to create the life they originally wanted with each other, instead of hiding their problems from each other until the problems become the most powerful force in the marriage. Statistics show that the average couple waits six years after the trouble begins before seeking help for their marriage, and that's probably five years and six months too late. If we used the same time frame to get help for physical ailments, we'd probably be dead.

Once we begin to withhold, most of us stop even noticing how we feel about our relationship—good, bad, indifferent—and just do all we can to endure it. *But marriage is designed to be more than an endurance contest.* It's the arena where partners can experience their greatest healing and joy! No, not every minute, sometimes not even every day. But most of the time, more good than bad, and if that's not happening, it's time to look for help to turn things around.

This morning I said to one of my daughters, "I'm a little embarrassed to let certain people know about such and such, and I'm even embarrassed to admit I'm embarrassed about that."

Admitting that I feel embarrassed is genuine, because I do. But I arrive at an even deeper level of honesty when I admit I'm embarrassed to be embarrassed.

Being genuine brings energy. Surprisingly, being genuine invigorates and energizes us. It adds vitality to our life and our relationships, whereas keeping secrets, hiding my truths, forcing people to try to read our minds or guess what's going on with us drains so much energy out of our relationships that eventually those relationships die. Being genuine brings responsibility, and it also brings freedom.

Polly and Perry are in love and happy as they begin their life together, caught up in Romantic Love. But after a time, they begin to move from the euphoria of Romantic Love into the disillusionment of the Power Struggle, and at that point they begin keeping secrets from each other.

Perry doesn't tell Polly he's spending $50 a week on lottery tickets, and Polly doesn't tell him about the $450 dress she bought, because they're supposed to be living on a budget, and if the truth comes out, Perry will blow up. Goodbye Romantic Love, Goodbye Authenticity; Hello Secrets, Hello Fear of Being Found Out. In time, when the reality can no longer be ignored because expense is far exceeding income, the truth begins to surface, at which point Perry and Polly will both feel deceived and lied to, and the relationship will be in danger of failing.

Or let's suppose that Jake spends every autumn weekend on the couch with a couple of six-packs and an endless supplies of munchies, zoned out on football, while his wife Josie fumes, preparing the next meal, looking after the kids, getting the week's laundry knocked out. She feels ignored and unvalued, but tries to rationalize her feelings: "All guys watch football, so I guess I'll just have to put up with it." Or, "If I complain, he'll call me a nagging wench, and I don't want the kids to hear that. I'll just keep my mouth shut."

But both of these marriages are headed for trouble, and unless somebody speaks up, eventually they will crack and fall apart. The partners in them will experience that draining away of *aliveness* and look for it somewhere else.

Secrets won't solve unhappiness. We don't keep secrets because we're dense or mean or naturally withholding. We do it because we start feeling unhappy, unsatisfied in our marriage. We remain unaware of the *toxicity* this withholding creates. We actually think we're protecting the relationship. Early on in our love relationships, we generally find it uncomfortable to hide parts of ourselves, because we really want to be genuine and authentic. That's our true nature before we felt a need to start building defenses.

Even though conflict is inevitable in a committed relationship, conflict scares us. So we rationalize, telling ourselves, "It's best to leave some things unsaid." We think we can sweep those secrets under the rug and keep them there, but they're like ants in the kitchen—as soon as we think we're rid of them and let up our guard, they start parading out again.

But we were real in the beginning. Romantic Love acts on us like a drug, and while under its influence we do talk in a genuine way with each other, because the "drug" allows us to *sustain the tension* and fear of letting the other person know our real feelings and thoughts. Part of the joy, in fact, is that feeling that "this is the first person who's ever really understood me." The "drug" of Romantic Love anesthetizes us enough that we can speak our truth without fear, and we do. We can spill our guts.

Allowing ourselves to be so vulnerable, we can't imagine that our partner would ever hurt us. And our partner doesn't hurt us, because our partner is also anesthetized on the same euphoric "drug." So, we get to tell all that good stuff we've wanted to pour out of our soul, and we have a listening ear in a partner who's taking it in, sympathizing, and really helping us feel completely accepted and normal—like we're really not crazy, validating us.

But when the "drug" wears off, we quit talking so honestly. We quit presenting our authentic selves. We give up our genuineness because of fear, and as we do that, we ward off that fear of losing our *aliveness* by using what energy we have left in dysfunctional ways, to try to make ourselves feel *alive* again. This is the process that kills the *aliveness* in our relationship.

The beginning of the dance. When my partner hurts my feelings or disappoints me about something, and I let him or her know I'm upset or hurt, if my partner comes back at me in a way that feels hurtful to me, I may then decide that I don't want to be so open the next time. I'd rather just hide my feelings and not let my partner know what's really going on with me.

Maybe she got mad at me and yelled at me or threatened me. Maybe she started crying and shamed me: "After all I have done for you!" Maybe she turned pitiful, martyrlike. Whatever she did, her behavior taught me that I don't want to be that open or that vulnerable any more.

Training ourselves to hold it in. So, in order to not be so open and vulnerable, I have to train myself to stop noticing when something bothers me. In the beginning, this is difficult. I have to find some way to trick myself, actually talk myself out of seeing or saying the reality of what bothers me. But as I trick myself in this way, I'm training myself to not notice. Eventually, I won't even know if I'm upset or if I'm hiding anything from my partner or myself. Not noticing has come to feel natural with me.

Let's go back to Polly and Perry. Now they are well into the Power Struggle, hiding their true selves from each other. And doing so is painful for them, because in the beginning they were able to be genuine with each other. Each one wanted the partner to see them as they really are, to accept them unconditionally. But money is a touchy subject at their house, so for the time being, at least, they prefer to let that touchy subject alone, avoiding the highly charged emotions it may stir up.

Perry goes on buying lottery tickets but hides the stubs, pretending he's not even interested when the winning numbers are announced. Polly brings home the new dress but hides it under the same plastic bag as her winter coat.

When she finally wears it to an event, if Perry says anything, she'll say, "This old thing? My sister gave it to me, she couldn't wear it any more."

If you want an example of authenticity, just watch a baby. Babies are entirely real and authentic. They come right out of their gut with everything. No one has any doubt when a baby is upset, or happy, or hungry, or needs a change, unless it's a baby that's been neglected or abused so long, it too has lost its beautiful authenticity.

As babies grow up, those who take care of them have to help them curtail a little bit of that letting-it-all-hang-out. But there are positive ways of teaching a baby to curtail it, and there are damaging ways. Children can be helped to postpone gratification just for a little while—delay getting their needs met—and sometimes that's quite necessary. But making a baby or a child learn to *hide* its true feelings is a damaging way, and *punishing* a child for being authentic is destructive.

Authenticity is lost. Unfortunately, by adulthood, if we learned to react to the threatening adults in our lives by *hiding* whatever was real to us, we allow our secrets to build up to such a toxic level that hardly anything authentic about us remains visible.

Suppose it's summertime, and after work Wynona's attorney husband William stops off at the neighborhood bar on his way home every afternoon for a couple of beers with the regulars there. Wynona, a stay-at-home mom, has had their three children (all under age six) the whole day, the air-conditioner has failed, and the temperature is pushing 95°.

The children look forward to seeing their dad, but when he walks in the door, instead of taking time to hug and notice them or Wynona, he goes straight to the kitchen, fixes himself a vodka martini, then carries it into the den, closes the door, and enjoys his drink—the third one of the afternoon—then gets on the computer for some interesting chats with "friends" until such time as he's ready for some family interaction.

Let's pass over the indications that William is fast moving into alcoholism. That's another problem, one that will have to be addressed eventually, if the marriage is to be saved. Right now Wynona doesn't disturb him, just goes on to feed the children their supper and give them their baths, waiting until William is ready to come out to eat. Lately he's been spending even more time than usual away from the house, and she's afraid he's seeing somebody else, though she hasn't said anything. A complaint about his emotional and physical unavailability could drive him straight to the mystery woman's arms.

At eight-thirty, when William does finally emerge, the casserole Wynona put together at four o'clock is dry as dust. He takes one bite, throws down his fork, slams out of the house, and tears out of the driveway headed who knows where. Wynona puts the children to bed and waits for him until she can't stay awake any longer, forgetting about supper, just eating a quart of chocolate ice cream to soothe her wounded soul. The next morning William is gone before Wynona or the children are up.

Every circumstance and event in this story is real, but nobody in this household has been genuine with anybody else about the truth that he or she perceives.

Distracting ourselves. In order for us to hide our truths, our feelings, our genuineness, we have to distract ourselves from what is real for us. We replace our authenticity with something else. That replacement could be work, drink, drugs, overeating, spending money, having affairs, overinvolvement with our kids, friends, families of origin, etc. All these replacements will help to anesthetize us, at least for a time, against our dissatisfaction and emotional pain. But the replacement is only a poor substitute for what we really need and want.

We're using *escapes* instead of talking to our partner about our unhappiness, our frustrations, our disappointments, our anger. We're killing the *aliveness*, yet what we want more than anything is to feel *alive* again. Crippled by our unwillingness or our inability to lay hold on our truth and express it, we reach out to something or someone other than our partner in the hope that that person or that thing will help us feel *alive* again.

For a while, after we turn to something or someone else, the energy of secrecy alone invigorates us, gives us that feeling we crave of being more *alive.* Yet when our escapes stop working—usually sex, money, alcohol, drugs, food—stop supplying enough energy to help us feel some *aliveness, then we add new energy by introducing risk, danger, and the heightened terror of being discovered* with our secret agendas.

For a time, this forbidden energy does add a higher buzz to whatever we are doing to escape our supposedly dead relationship. That's why affairs feel so energizing. Drinking or drugging feels the same way for a time. We hide those behaviors, knowing our partner would disapprove, and the hiding adds heightened energy to the picture. It's a dysfunctional energy, but it feels better than deadness. When your relationship feels dead, any energy feels better than no energy at all.

As we drain the *aliveness* out of our relationship, our partner will also notice that the relationship feels dead and become miserable, too. And suppose my partner is someone who doesn't say anything about the misery, because he fears that I might get upset or respond to him or her in a way that might feel shaming. So, my partner just hides what's going on with him, feeling dead and numbed out in our relationship, and pretty soon we have a relationship that really is dead, and we blame each other for that.

By that time, neither of us can say which partner started this dance. All we know is that something has sapped the relationship of its *aliveness*. Most of us never understand that the difficulties started when one or both of us stopped talking to the other about what was real and troublesome in our experience with each other.

And then we hate the dead relationship, because we don't want to be in a partnership that feels dead. We look at our partner, and our partner feels dead to us. It gets progressively worse, until there's no life left in the relationship at all. The only life we feel in ourselves is whatever we are doing on the side, secretively, and that's the life of an emotional pauper.

Cultivating a secret life in order to feel *alive* is a childlike way of functioning in what should be mature adult relationships. We tell ourselves that the relationship has died, convince ourselves we're completely within our rights when we look for something else that will make us feel more *alive* than staying in a dead relationship. We refuse to look at or see how *we killed the relationship*, blaming our partner instead. We can actually make ourselves believe it, convince other people too. "The love just isn't there any more," we'll say, feeling sorry for ourselves, looking for an escape or even already out the back door.

Where the healing truth lies. No matter how convinced we may be that speaking our truth will finish off the relationship for sure, so long as we're unwilling to deal in a genuine way with our partner, we're killing the relationship ourselves by withholding our truth, honesty, and authentic energies from it.

I often tell clients in therapy, "If you're in a relationship that can tolerate only one person's truth, it's not much of a relationship, and it cannot grow in a healthy direction."

Early on, when we try to tell our partner we don't like certain things that happen between us, sometimes our partner responds in a hurtful way. But instead of going to our partner and telling our truth right then—"I told you something yesterday that I felt very vulnerable even saying, and you came back at me in a very hurtful way"—we don't do that.

Instead, we shut up, or act out, or rage, or do something else rather than tell our truth. We fall back on our childhood defenses, or the ones we learned from watching our parents operate. And any time we react with our defenses, we close down the *aliveness* in the relationship. As we give up our genuineness— our words and feelings begin to not match up with our behaviors.

If I let you hurt me, and don't address that, then I'm contributing to the death of our relationship. If I do address you when you hurt me, and you respond in a hurtful way, I need to be adult enough to go back and address that, too. Keeping the authentic dialogue going preserves the *aliveness* in the relationship. *It's only when we stop addressing what is going on right here, right now in our relationship, that we kill it.*

Many of us grew up with parents who never moved into adult functioning. I watched my own parents live and die on this earth, never functioning on a higher emotional level than very young children. Nobody wants to be a child forever, but sometimes we need help in leaving emotional childhood behind. The goal of all of this relationship work is to GROW UP—to have alive, grown-up, connected relationships.

We need to be able to talk to each other as adults, in an honest, genuine way, and if the reception isn't favorable, we need to *hold onto our truth* and continue talking until we reach some resolution. Some pauses during this process may be necessary to allow partners to remain present and appropriate with each other. The main thing is, don't let the process end, because the process itself is healing.

A partner who's stuck. "But what can I do?" you may be saying. "I want our relationship to get better, and I'm willing to change, but my partner refuses to talk and refuses to learn how to stay open, honest, and genuine."

Remember, we can't change others. We can only change ourselves. What we ultimately seek in a long-term, committed, love relationship is an emotionally safe connecting energy between two people. It's an energy that comes from *inside*, not from *outside*—from a generous-spirited giving of my real self to my partner, from my much-desired acceptance of the same kind of self-giving from my mate, a relationship with both people being real and genuine. Neither partner needs to hide their authenticity, because the relationship can tolerate both realities, that high level of honesty and being real with each other.

In relationship therapy, it's important to remember that neither partner is the "patient." The relationship is the focus, and the goal is to do whatever will lead to the healthiest, most connected relationship. So perhaps if you present it to your partner in that way—"It's not you or me that needs fixing, it's our relationship that needs help, and we both want it to be better"— maybe he or she will be willing to learn these skills.

If not, then you have a decision to make as to how you intend to live out the rest of your life in terms of that relationship. Will you choose to stay in gridlock, expressing only what your partner or your family wants to hear, or will you choose to grow by telling your truth in as gentle a way as possible while working on correcting your own defensive behaviors and finding better understandings about your differences?

When a couple comes to relationship therapy, one of the two may already have made up his or her mind that the relationship is over, there's no fixing it, and all he or she wants is out. In my experience, this adamant stance—"I want out! There's no fixing this relationship!"—only happens when one or both partners already have another partner or prospects of a new one, or when an addiction—alcohol, drugs, gambling—has set in or an old addiction has strengthened its hold. It usually doesn't take long for that fact to surface.

But even those powerful exit points don't have to force an end to the marriage, unless one partner, or both, is unwilling to change, learn, and work on the relationship. Under the right circumstances affairs can be forgiven, alcoholics and addicts can get help for recovery, and gamblers can find support-group help, clearing the way for healing work to begin in the relationship. Of course it isn't just a case of forgive and forget. Amends will have to be made, and behavioral changes must replace promises. But when such things happen, marriages have been saved and families made whole.

I tell partners, "You don't need to *want* to work on the relationship, nor do you have to have a *good attitude*. All you have to be is *willing*, which means open to learn, workable, and ready to do things differently in the marriage."

After Romantic Love, we have to recreate connection with our partner, this time within the framework of a *real* world. This can happen in a lasting way by making sure both partners are being authentic—living their value systems, matching up their words with their behaviors—understanding that no one can live in two opposing worlds and be genuine at the same time. Being genuine is a necessary component to having a real and connected life with a long-term, committed partner.

Chapter 12

Your Partner Is As Emotionally Healthy As You Can Tolerate

"I'm not sure I know who this person is any more."

It's human nature: if I'm unhappy in our relationship, I expect *you* to change. That's just the way people are—we seldom look at ourselves first. When we realize we're unhappy in a partner relationship, we quickly point out all the changes that our partner needs to make in order for us to have a happy relationship again: "I'm all right, Jack, it's you that needs fixing!"

When something goes wrong between me and my partner, I sincerely believe I'm only reacting to my partner's hurtful behavior. I assume that if that hurtful behavior is stopped, then I can be sweet and pleasant again, too. We believe that the partner has to shape up before we can put away our defensive behaviors.

Unfortunately, relationships aren't that simple. *What neither partner can see is their unconscious agendas working underground.* Actually, two forces must be reckoned with when partners reach this place in their relationship:

1) The Power Struggle—each partner is trying to be his/her separate, different self, assert his or her will, and gain personal power over the other; and

2) The Personal Psyche—each partner's emotional state, plus defense mechanisms, which determine whether healing of the relationship is possible, the amount of work required to bring it about, the degree of healing that can take place at any particular time, and how fast that healing can occur.

Revisiting the Power Struggle. To understand the Power Struggle, we must look at its unique components. We've touched on it briefly before, acknowledging that according to Harville Hendrix's IMAGO theory, the Power Struggle is the second stage of a primary love relationship. It's supposed to begin, and it's supposed to end. In a culture that allows couples to be attracted to and choose their own partners, this Power Struggle is a predictable and completely normal stage of any marriage. If both partners stay alive and stay together, the Power Struggle arrives as the Romantic Love stage winds down.

Recapping further, in its early stages, the Power Struggle manifests with disillusionment: "My partner is not who I thought he or she really was," "My partner reminds me of other people who hurt me" (usually family members), "I'm not as happy as I had hoped to be," "My partner doesn't listen to me any more," "My partner doesn't try to please me as she or he once did," etc.

When the relationship arrives at this point we become very focused on how *different* the two of us are and conclude that our choice of a partner was really a mistake. And, sadly, for many couples the relationship ends right there. Having learned very little about how to make a relationship work, they bail out of that marriage and start looking for somebody who will be "right." When that "right" person shows up, the cycle will start all over again, with Romantic Love followed by the onset of the Power Struggle—you see where I'm going with this.

Disillusionment can equal opportunity. When the Power Struggle begins, instead of deciding that the relationship is over and divorce is the only way to go, a wonderful opportunity is presenting itself to the couple. If they will make the commitment to go to work on the relationship, both partners can learn a great deal and find deeper satisfaction in that relationship and life. The Power Struggle is a big "STOP" sign. The relationship has gone as far as it will go, unless both partners address some vital issues. And they can rarely do this without becoming educated, guided, and supported by a trained professional, who is what Frank Pittman, M.D., refers to as "a friend to the marriage relationship."

Suppose a partner has begun to work most of the time, or gets caught up in too many involvements away from home, or is alcoholic or depends on other chemicals, or is having an affair, or withdraws energy from the partner relationship in some other way to invest it elsewhere. What happens with the other partner? Initially that partner often pursues the unavailable mate; after a time, however, he or she distances also, and now there's a definite *disconnect* between the two. Perhaps this distancing partner has also been overinvolved with something besides the relationship—kids, friends, work, community activities, spending money, going to school, being sick, sleeping a lot, etc.

It really doesn't matter which partner begins pulling away from the relationship. Someone will; it's predictable. None of us is equipped to stay as close to anyone over an extended period of time as when we're first in the throes of Romantic Love.

We got hurt before, we don't want to feel hurt again. Early on, in our families of origin, all of us were hurt emotionally in one way or another, and those hurts are still there deep down inside. As a result, we carry with us into adult life a genuine but often unrecognized fear of getting as close to another person as one must be in order to live healthily with one partner in a trustful, long-term, connected relationship.

During Romantic Love, we reveled in the belief that the wonderful partner who'd come into our life couldn't or wouldn't ever mortally wound us. We believed that we could trust that partner absolutely, placing our total emotional safety in the other person's hands. We are able to do this fearlessly in the Romantic Love stage, because both partners are under the euphoric spell of the endorphins being produced in our brains. We are "high" on love!

Without this absolute trust in one another, we would never commit to another person for a lifetime, and this level of trust holds a component of the unconditional love we all long for. We dream of being able to free-fall into our lover's arms and always be caught and cherished for who we are.

Why does the shine wear off? If we start out in Romantic Love with such high hopes, such wonderful expectations, why can't it last forever? It can't last forever because:

1) We still have old unresolved emotional baggage that we drag with us into our relationships, and
2) We have to *grow* in order to evolve into all that we were originally designed to be.

The dusty old trunks full of childhood junk stay in the closet during the honeymoon and often for several years, but eventually they have to be opened, sorted through, and cleaned out.

Human beings are social creatures by nature. We all want close, connected relationships, and we love how those feel. Being in a close, intimate relationship for an extended time is more than our psyches can tolerate, however, and our old defenses around control begin to kick in. This is the essence of the Power Struggle in a committed love relationship.

That being so, the Power Struggle is tailor-made to help us get old unresolved issues healed, with the goal of finally growing into the emotionally healthy partner capable of experiencing the love we have always wanted. Our desire for this love never leaves us. We will continue to long for it and pursue it until we have actually experienced it, or at least until we have realistic hopes that we can and will experience it at some point.

The clarity we're missing is the understanding that we must all *stretch and grow* into the person who is emotionally healthy enough to experience this love.

Nobody ever told us the journey to lifelong love with a partner required us to *grow*. Our cultural myths, plus Romantic Love, convinced us that we've arrived at this place of emotional health and love by connecting with the "right" partner. But when the Power Struggle breaks out, it leads us to believe we've wound up with the "wrong" partner instead. Yet both stages are necessary to bring us to the *place of growth*.

Who's in charge of me, anyway? Now let's go back to that statement, "Early on, in our families of origin, all of us were hurt emotionally in one way or another, and those hurts are still there deep down inside." What I'm talking about here is *actual control* versus *perceived control*. As children, of course we felt controlled, because we were. We don't ever forget what that felt like.

Then, as adults in partner relationships, when the Power Struggle begins, we re-experience the feeling of being controlled that we felt in childhood with a parent. We're programmed to interpret control that way, and at an unconscious level it feels familiar to us. When our partner begins exerting some sort of control on us in adulthood, we intercept the new control and superimpose our old impression and experience of control over it, making the new control feel like the old control we experienced as a child. That is our *perceived control*.

Let me share an experience of my own. My father was alcoholic, very abusive and aggressive. My husband, on the other hand, is thoughtful and sensitive most of the time. Years ago, he might ask me where I would like to go out for dinner, suggesting steaks or seafood. What a nice guy!

Yet, in my head, I heard, "You cannot have Mexican or Italian food, because I want steaks or seafood." What I heard in my head had nothing to do with my husband's intent, what he was suggesting, or what was in his head. He was actually trying to be thoughtful and offer some ideas, while I was feeling controlled and repressed by his simple suggestion.

Why in the world was that? It was because in those days I was still programmed to believe I did not have choices and was not allowed to make up my own mind about anything, because my father never allowed that, and I was still playing by the old home-based rules. So I superimposed my father's control and lack of consideration for my wishes over my husband's thoughtful suggestions and ended up feeling the same control and manipulation from my husband that I felt from my father. And just deciding where to go out for dinner became a power struggle for me. This is another example of how our unfinished issues from childhood affect our relationships today.

When parental control goes awry. Part of the natural order of raising a child is for parents to have a significant amount of control in order to keep the child safe and teach the child about life. None of us had perfect parents, and none of us became perfect parents, so the natural process of raising a child gets interrupted by the dysfunction of each of our parents.

Some of us grew up in homes where we were noticeably controlled by one or both parents hitting, yelling, slapping, being critical, comparing us to others, demeaning, punishing, withholding affection, bullying and threatening us, shaming us, and teaching us a fear of closeness—not surprising, since we couldn't trust them to be close to us without hurting us. One part of us loved these parents, but another part of us was and still may be very angry and resentful of their disregard for us.

Then there are those of us who grew up in homes with parents who controlled us more subtly. They were terribly busy, had no time for us, weren't available to us physically, emotionally, or both. Maybe they had to work very hard to make ends meet, maybe they were ill, depressed, or not there for us in some other way (divorce or death, perhaps).

As children of such parents we perceived them as trying hard, and we excused their dismissal of us and rationalized their busyness and unavailability to us. We sympathized with them, felt sorry for them, didn't want to disappoint or upset them because they had "enough to worry about," couldn't allow ourselves to feel angry with them when they left us through divorce or death (which they "couldn't avoid"), or felt sorry for them because they'd had a "hard life" and didn't get help for themselves ("poor thing").

Other family dramas. Some parents who had little or no satisfactory relationship with their adult partner put all their energy into their children, expecting in return to be taken care of emotionally by those children. Their theme song goes like this: "After all I've done for these kids, making me happy seems like the least they can do for me. " These powerless, pitiful parents are often sick much of the time, addicted to chemicals, or behaving in other ways that worry their families. A part of us loves them, but another part has always felt burdened by and totally controlled by them. If we have families of origin like this, we've come to believe, usually unconsciously, that all close relationships are just too burdensome and require too much energy, so we don't want to and probably believe we can't have any love relationship of our own.

Adults who emerge from all these family dramas will bring huge unresolved issues from childhood into their adult love relationships. No matter how often or how vehemently we tell ourselves, "I'll never be like my mom, or my dad!" or "I'm determined my family won't be anything like my own horrible one was!" we find ourselves recreating the same old scenes.

What we've failed to take into account is the power of the Unconscious Mind. Old family-of-origin stuff just floats around in there and seeps out of us onto our close relationships and the people we love. And in order to have the relationships we crave and help our wounded spirits heal, we have to resurrect all that old family stuff, examine it, allow ourselves to feel any pain we've been denying, then let as much of it go as possible. And if we can stay together and be caring partners throughout, so much the better for us both and for our relationship.

In putting together these Twelve Foundation Stones for committed love relationships, our work calls for us to take a look at how satisfied or dissatisfied we are with our relationships, honestly examine the roles we've been playing in them, listen to how our partner and kids experience us, and be willing to grow by altering our defensive interactions with these people we love, so that we can stop hurting them, get some healing around our own wounding, and become emotionally safe enough for them to connect with us.

Old fears revive. *Until we work on our issues within the Power Struggle, whatever control we felt as a child, we will perceive our partner as having that much or even more control over us.* In trying to sustain an adult, long-term love relationship, our old fears about control revive, and although we couldn't resist effectively as a child, we now begin to act the old drama out on our partner—all that old resistance, plus any new defenses we've picked up over the years.

Let's suppose Art, who had an obviously controlling father and a powerless mother, marries Amy, whose parents were basically unavailable and uninvolved in her life as a child. Perhaps they were neglectful, or perhaps circumstance required their attention elsewhere. Both Art and Amy grew up feeling controlled, Art from noticeable control and Amy from circumstances. Being as resourceful as most children are, they adapted. They learned emotional defenses to protect themselves from feeling so powerless and unnurtured. And as adults, they will continue to use their protective defenses with their partner, in either an obvious or a subtle way.

Chances are that Amy never labeled her childhood experience with her parents as controlling. In fact, because there was so little parental involvement, she probably essentially raised herself, which made her feel powerful, as if she had a great deal of control over her life. But because she was a child and needed parents to show her about life, she grew up shy and lacking confidence, or she may have compensated with an inflated, artificial confidence in herself.

Art, who probably understands quite well that he felt controlled, is determined to make sure that doesn't happen again in any other relationship.

Art alleviates his fears about being controlled by aggressively and rigidly controlling others, like his dad before him.

So here now are Art and Amy, both of whom emerged from childhood unable to remain close to anyone for long. Their psyches will make sure, however, that they feel power somewhere in their relationships, and their defense systems will kick in to help them accomplish that.

It's Saturday afternoon at the Bijou. I've talked often about the "movie" we have running in our heads and project onto a partner. Watching couples struggle to feel powerful in their relationships is like watching a video of their childhood. Art, who felt very controlled as a child, will perceive his partner Amy as being very controlling, and his old defenses will be set into motion, so that he reacts to his *perceived* control from Amy by acting out against her. Amy will perceive Art as being critical, demanding, shaming, and ungrateful, and his behavior will probably confirm her view of him.

Amy's behavior will match the "control movie" running in Art's head, and he will defend against it just as he did as a child—by fighting, fleeing, throwing tantrums, storming out, freezing up, getting quiet, or whatever worked for him.

Furthermore, because Amy also felt very controlled as a child, at an unconscious level, Art's behavior will feel *normal* to her and will match enough of the "control movie" running in her head that Amy will accept it as a *natural* part of a relationship. She then goes on to defend herself against it just as she did as a child—by submitting, freezing up, numbing out, throwing tantrums, running away, fighting, arguing, or whatever worked for her as a child.

And then Art will come to perceive Amy as a nag, a crybaby, powerless, pitiful, totally empty-headed, a drama queen; and her behavior will bear out his description. The old "movie" or "video" is playing, and until somebody rewrites the script, it never ends happily.

Why behaviors persist or disappear. To sum up, unless a behavior in either partner is serving a purpose, such as reminding one's Old Brain of old unresolved issues that need healing, it will soon disappear in the relationship, because one partner or the other won't tolerate the behavior. So long as each partner is bringing old stuff to the table, however, all that old stuff has to be acknowledged and worked through in order for a new, healthy, connected partnership to form.

Joyce Buckner has summed this dynamic up neatly: "We don't pair up with a partner who is more or less evolved than we." No matter how much we'd like to believe otherwise, we didn't marry this "impossible" person by accident. We pair up with a partner who carries about the same amount of woundedness from childhood as we. It's as if Nature planned it that way, sending us partners who can help us heal, if we will both welcome the invitation and stay for the whole party.

Because my own family was so obviously "sick," my husband and I accepted that I was the partner with "the most problems." For a long time I went along with this assumption, until I began to grow into healthier beliefs, at which point I began to question the "squeaky clean" of my husband's family. And a time came in our work as a couple—as that time always will come—when my husband had to examine his own relationships and family-of-origin history. As we both began to recognize that the family he came from was just as "sick," or as dysfunctional as mine, I have to admit this discovery brought me great comfort. His family just hid their shortcomings better!

We do our growing up together. So long as we fail to grow up emotionally, so long as either of us remains in our emotional child state, *we really cannot allow our partner much growth*, because we aren't equipped to handle it. We're still operating out of our old defenses, and they won't work—won't be tolerated by an emotionally healthy partner. Those of us who came from controlling homes designed our defense systems to cope with people who inhabited adult bodies but emotionally had never grown past being a child. Our parents lived like that, and so did their parents, and their parents, *ad infinitum.*

So, when partners begin to work through their issues *together*, they begin *slowly* to grow up emotionally. I say "slowly," because our psyches cannot tolerate fast growth. A decision to move into new ways of doing relationships and become willing to alter our behaviors requires our psyche to reshape our entire defense systems into healthier ways of coping and interacting. Defenses can be let go of, eventually, but changing *instantly* from operating within a structure of childlike emotions to a system of adult, healthy coping mechanisms would cause a breakdown of the whole organism.

Getting "worse" can be getting better. So we must progress in tiny baby steps, with partners moving ahead by small increments, almost simultaneously. If one partner moves too quickly, the relationship will be disrupted. That's why if only one partner is in therapy and growing, the relationship will usually get worse. The partner in therapy is most likely getting healthier in his or her ability to operate in close relationships, and whatever problems have clung to the relationship are going to demand resolution. The healthier that partner gets, the less dysfunction he or she will be willing to tolerate.

Yet this "getting worse" can actually be what needs to happen! The "getting worse" partner who hasn't been willing to learn new, healthier ways of being in relationship is being sent a message that the old ways are dead, and change is happening. He or she can stay stuck in unhappiness and the Power Struggle, or else decide to participate in the journey to emotional growth and health.

The same is true when one partner's dysfunction goes so far off the *other* end of the spectrum as to become life-threatening—usually involving some form of addiction. The relationship will get worse, because the better-functioning partner's psychic limits have been reached. All relationships can tolerate a certain amount of dysfunction, but too much dysfunction will devastate any system.

Collapse of a relationship is not always a calamity. Many times a relationship is crying out for drastic change, as one partner decides to stop putting up with abusive behavior. The relationship will be devastated, but for a positive end. It needs to be devastated, at least in the old shape. Transformation is trying to happen.

Dillon and Diedra had been married for thirty years, and throughout their marriage the drinking of both had gradually increased. Eventually a business breakdown, coupled with a health crisis, forced Dillon to come to grips with his alcoholism. He joined Alcoholics Anonymous, embracing sobriety enthusiastically and working hard to maintain his recovery.

Soon Deidra was complaining: "I don't know who this person is any more." She chose to separate from Dillon without asking for a divorce, moved to a city some distance away, and rented an apartment, living there on her own for several months before deciding that her better course was to reunite with Dillon and learn to live with the new person he was becoming. And in the end Deidra, too, acknowledged that she needed help for her own drinking problem.

The collapse of a relationship may be the catalyst that allows partners, with help and education, to reorganize their relationship into a functional, genuinely loving partnership. In many instances the collapse of the old is essential for a new beginning—for example, when so much damage has been done that neither partner can recover under the old system. Just about everything in the old system must change, but again, *very slowly*, as each partner learns to regroup, tolerate the new, and stretch into the potential that was always there, just blocked by old unexamined baggage.

This work takes patience, practice, and perseverance. If both partners can be encouraged to remember that it's not one or the other who needs "fixing," it's the relationship itself, they may choose to stay with the task long enough to experience the great benefits that will come from building a marriage that is "we" based.

As the exploration and transformation progresses, on the solid awareness of the Twelve Foundation Stones, the relationship doesn't become easy—no relationship is—but it becomes the sacred space where we can find the love for which we have always longed.

Epilogue

At some point in my own process in therapy, I began to change. I began to tolerate less and less of the "old way" of doing our marriage, carrying the emotional load of our relationship, while my husband kept busy working to "fix" our emotions in concrete ways.

I posed a particular question to my husband on many occasions: "Why can't you learn how to communicate, read, journal, attend Twelve Step meetings, go to therapy, and analyze your addictions as I have mine, so our relationship can become better?" (Note that I didn't say I had arrived at a high level of mental health or even entirely healthy ways of relating).

His answer came by way of comparison to a situation taken from the Old Testament, and here is the way he related that to me in a letter:

> It's like the story of the Pharaoh of Egypt and the Jewish slaves—me being the Pharaoh, you being the slaves. For you, this new way of life is as if Moses, the deliverer, has come to set you free. You're excited to be learning about freedom, hungry to learn more. You're more willing to participate in anything. You're happy to read anything that makes you more free, less bound. It's as if the restrictions and rules that have held you back all these years are gone, and you're starved to reach out for more and more of this free way to live.
>
> "On the other hand, here I am, like Pharaoh, who has always come and gone as he pleased—never been questioned about anything—never had to look at his actions and how they affected other people, never had to explain to anyone what he really thinks, needs, or feels, if he ever even knew what he felt. Nobody before confronted him with different realities, nobody ever said it's a new day, the old ways are gone. And when that day came, poor old Pharaoh couldn't adapt.
>
> Now, here I am being told to listen to other people in my life and how they feel about what I do. I'm being told things to read, so I can learn a new way to act, feel, express feelings, and worst of all, discover what is and has been

wrong with me and my relationships with others. This is hard for the "King," the "Pharaoh," the "Authority," to take, to understand, to accept. Yet I know if I don't do it, I will suffer the same end as Pharaoh—lonely, broken, and left in the dust behind.

All these years I've been under the delusion that things were great, wonderful, that everyone I dealt with had the same freedom and fun I was having, or thought I was having. Now, I'm being called to look at what I've done and how it impacts others, facing the fact that I wasn't as fair or as wonderful as I thought.

I've had to recognize that at times I've been mean, uncaring, selfish, self-centered, and a downright dictator based on my own pleasures and what I assumed were other peoples' desires and feelings. I realize that I was all wrong. Now I'm doing it, doing as you ask, and as I read, talk about my true feelings, attend therapy, and go to Twelve Step programs, I recognize that who I thought I was and what I thought was happening really wasn't anything like the truth of what you and our kids were experiencing from me.

Now, it feels to me as if I'm putting shackles on myself, becoming the bound slave, in comparison to how it used to be. This reading and talking is hard for me. I've never had to do it before, and it comes so slow, so hard, hurting so much. I'm lazy, procrastinate about making the time to do these things……."

Do you see that he was asking me to be patient with him, to understand, to give him time? The crucial difference between him and Pharaoh was that he was *trying*. He was *making the effort*, although his pace wasn't necessarily the same as mine. I was grateful to him for letting me know how he felt, what a struggle he was having, for in doing so he helped me to be more caring and patient with him.

So, as you can see, my husband and I are certainly no example of the 'perfectly happy married' couple. What we do provide for each other is a lot of *hope* as we continue to talk and express our worlds to each other and teach each other what makes us feel safe in our relationship. The two of us have made a long, mutually difficult journey that I wouldn't trade for anything, striving to stay connected and learning to pace ourselves as together we learn a new way to live and build the life that we have always wanted.

Suggested
Additional Reading

Beveridge, Martha. *Loving Your Partner Without Losing Yourself*, California: Hunter House Publishers, 2001

Bradshaw, John. *Family Secrets*, New York: Bantam Books, 1996.

Bradshaw, John. *Creating Love*, New York: Bantam Books, 1994.

Christensen, Andrew and Jacobson, Neil S. *Reconcilable Differences*, New York: The Guilford Press, 2000.

Cox, Fran and Louis. *A Conscious Life*. Berkeley, CA: Conari Press, 1996.

Dutton, Donald. *The Batterer, A Psychological Profile*, New York: Basic Books, 1995.

Gottman, John. *Raising An Emotionally Intelligent Child*, Simon & Schuster: New York, 1997.

Gratch, Alon. *If Men Could Talk, Here's What They'd Say*, Boston: Little, Brown and Company, 2001.

Hendrix, Harville. *Getting the Love You Want*, New York: Harper Perennial, 1988.

Hendrix, Harville. *Keeping the Love You Find*, New York: Pocket Books, 1992.

Jennings, James. *The Little Red Book, Revised Edition*, Minnesota: Hazelden Foundation, 1986

Karen, Robert. *Becoming Attached*, New York: Oxford University press, 1998.

LeBoutillier, Megan. *"NO" is a Complete Sentence*, New York: Ballantine Books, 1995.

Love, Pat. *The Emotional Incest Syndrome*, New York: Bantam Books, 1990.

Love, Pat. *The Truth About Love,* New York: Fireside Book, Simon & Schuster 2001.

Mellody, Pia. *Facing Codependence*, New York: HarperSanFrancisco, 1989.

Mellody, Pia. *Facing Love Addiction*, New York: HarperSanFrancisco, 1992.

Miller, Angelyn. *The Enabler*, New York: Ballantine Books, 1988.

Miller, Alice. *The Drama of the Gifted Child*, New York: Basic Books, Revised & Updated Edition, 1994.

Miller, Alice. *Thou Shalt Not Be Aware*, Translated by Hildegarde and Hunter Hannum, New York: Meridian Book 1986.

Pittman, Frank. *Grow Up!: How Taking Responsibility Can Make You A Happy Adult*, New York: Golden Books, 1998.

Real, Terrence. *I Don't Want To Talk About It*, New York: Scribner, 1997.

Real, Terrence. *How Do I Get Through To You?,* New York: Scribner, 2002.

Rogers, Carl. *On Becoming A Person*, New York: Mariner Books, 1961

Twerski, Abraham and Naaken, Craig. *Addictive Thinking* and *The Addictive Personality*, two volumes in one, New York: MJF Books, 1990 and 1988 respectively.

Twerski, Abraham. *Substance-Abusing High Achievers*, New Jersey: Jason Aronson, Inc., 1998.

Wesselmann, Debra. *The Whole Parent*, New York: Insight Books, 1998.

Wolinsky, Stephen. *Trances People Live*, Connecticut: Bramble Company, 1991.

Ordering Information
For Saundra Dickinson's Book and Teaching Videos:

"**LOVE THAT WORKS**" full set of teaching **CDs** has **20** sessions, 25 minutes each
Item #1 Presented by Saundra Dickinson.......**$125.00**

1) "Relationship Myths and Realities"	2) "Let's Talk About Feelings"
3) "Romantic Love and the Power Struggle"	4) "How Each Partner Defends During the Power Struggle"
5) "Healthy Communication"	6) "Learning to Work With Anger"

7) "Emotional Safety in Committed Love Relationships"

8) "Resolving Conflict in Relationships"	9) "What is Reality?"
10) "Emotional Blackmail"	11) "Healthy Boundaries"
12) "Stepping Out of the Victim Box"	13) "How Kids Act Out Their Parents' Problems"

14) "Partnering vs. Parenting"

15) "The High Risk of a Child Centered Home"

16) "Making Marriage A WE Proposition"

17) "Learning About Projection"

18) "Getting Mom & Dad Out of the China Closet"

19) "Addictions: If You Really Loved Me, You'd Stop That"

20) "Your Partner is As Emotionally Healthy As You Can Tolerate"

Item #2 The book, <u>LOVE THAT WORKS: The Twelve Foundation Stones</u>
By Saundra Dickinson........**$15.95**

Any of the above may be ordered by phone, fax, or through our website @ :

www.saundradickinson.com

To order by fax, make a copy of the order form and fax to:
Saundra Dickinson FAX: 281-358-5890
Telephone: 281-358-3299

We take **MC, VISA, & AMEX, CHECK, OR MONEY ORDER**

Watch "Love That Works" TV series every
Monday evening at 9:00pm on
Kingwood Cable, channel 23,
or even better, *order the CD's of these 20
teaching sessions.*

ORDER FORM

Name_____

Address_____

City_____State_____Zip_____

Area code + phone number_____

Visa or MasterCard #_____Exp_____

Signature of card holder_____

Email address_____

▶ For purchases of more than one
item, regular Ground Delivery fee is
charged, plus 5% handling fee.

Please select from the Item Nos. above and list each, plus quantities, price per Item No. & total.

Item #	Quantities	Price/Item

Total for Items_____$_____
Texas Residents add 8.25% Tax
                    $_____
S & H for one Item $____ 2.95_____
Total for order____$_____

Saundra speaks to audiences throughout the year on these topics:

▶ To schools on communication, positive discipline, parenting issues, and teaching kids responsibility and accountability.

▶ To churches on increasing the spiritual and emotional aspects of marriage and family, including parenting and couple relationships.

▶ To the Armed Forces on how to maintain a healthy marriage and family while being separated geographically or having to relocate.

▶ To hospitals on stress and handling grief, anger, and fears.

▶ Topics can be tailored to fit your group or special occasion.

▶▶ **Invite this talented professional, Saundra Dickinson, to custom design a topic of your choice and present it for your next fundraiser or meeting!** ◀◀

www.saundradickinson.com